Reclaimed

Finding Your Identity after Marital Betrayal

Reclaimed

Finding Your Identity after Marital Betrayal

Your
30-DAY
Personal Journey

STEPHANIE BROERSMA

REDEMPTION
PRESS

Published by Redemption Press, PO Box 427, Enumclaw, WA 98022

Toll Free (844) 2REDEEM (273-3336)

Redemption Press is honored to present this title in partnership with the author. The views expressed or implied in this work are those of the author. Redemption Press provides our imprint seal representing design excellence, creative content, and high quality production.

Names have been changed to protect privacy.
Logo Design by Lisa DenBleyker, Lynden, WA
Printed in the United States.

For more information, contact:
Reclaimed Ministry Stephanie Broersma
P.O. Box 569
Lynden, Washington, 98264
United States of America

To learn more about Reclaimed Ministry and related materials,
visit: www.reclaimedministry.com
@reclaimedministry

ISBN 13: 978-1-68314-987-3 (Paperback)
978-1-68314-988-0 (ePub)
978-1-68314-989-7 (Mobi)

Library of Congress Catalog Card Number: 2019907984

Table of Contents

Dedication

To my sweet older sister, Traci, my biggest cheerleader.
I can hear you still, cheering me on from heaven.
To the women who have trusted me, and continue to trust me,
with their stories.
And to my husband, Tim, who continues to pursue me daily.

FOREWORD

Catherine Theriault

"*I will give you beauty* for ashes." No words could be truer for Stephanie Broersma.

Reclaimed is an invitation into a beautiful story of redemption, a story of how one shattered woman allowed her Savior to pick up the pieces of her heart and mend them back together with grace and dignity. Stephanie's brutal honesty allows the reader into the raw pain that accompanies infidelity. She masterfully articulates the confusion, denial, shame, and anger that came from her own story of brokenness to freedom.

In a world where no one talks about the dirty secrets surrounding the aftermath of an affair, Stephanie dares to put into words what every woman feels. Her journey of healing is a gift to every person who has ever felt the wounds of marital betrayal. This book is a healing balm, a life changer for the woman who has tasted the tears of infidelity. It's a survival guide and a road map to the truth of what is possible when a woman is reclaimed by Jesus Christ to live the life she was created to live.

As a pastor's wife, Catherine Theriault was on staff at a large church, leading, directing, and counseling those within the church. Currently, she is a life coach and parent aide at Arizona Baptist Children's Services.

A Normal Girl with an Unexpected Story

Come and listen, all you who fear God;
let me tell you what he has done for me.

Psalm 66:16

My childhood was textbook, according to what North American society standards were and how ordinary families were perceived on TV in the 1980s. I grew up in a Christian home with two parents, Paul and Cheryl, who were and still are, forty years later, dedicated to family, work, and providing stability within our home unit. The greatest gift my parents gave me was the blessing of a two-parent home. Yes, I heard and saw fights like any normal married couple has in their years together, but our home was always secure, safe, and loving.

Girl Meets Boy

Tim Broersma and I had no intention of dating in high school. That didn't stop me from admiring him. As a freshman, I thought he was so cute that I even wrote him a love letter. Oh, to be young and naïve! I'm not sure what my intentions were in writing that silly letter, but his sister Becky was my best friend, and being new to the school, I generally trusted what she had to say. She talked a lot about her brother, and when Tim finally tried to ask me out, I didn't give him the chance to complete his sentence. "No," I blurted. "Becky said to say no!" I'm so grateful for that advice.

We traveled our separate ways through high school. I had just graduated when our paths crossed again. This time, something sparked between us, and we began a "just friends" phase that lasted about three to four months. I worked at Goldie's Bar and Grill that summer, and to my surprise, I often found notes, gifts, or Tim by my car, waiting for me to finish my shift. We spent many hours at the diner Shari's, sitting over a cup of coffee or hot chocolate, discussing life, breakups, and faith.

We spent countless hours chatting the summer evenings away just as friends. It wasn't until I moved down to Seattle for college that our relationship changed, and the thought of being apart became unbearable.

Marriage to Honeymoon in Paris

Tim and I dated for a few years before he asked me to marry him. From the proposal to the wedding ceremony, everything was perfect. We honeymooned in Paris, then traveled to Scandinavia over our first-year anniversary with the semiprofessional barbershop quartet Tim was a part of.

Time passed, and we were secure in our jobs, living comfortably in our first home. It was a fixer-upper, but it was ours. Tim's five-year plan—to hold off on children for five years—lasted all of three years, when our firstborn daughter, Addison, arrived. After some hard discussions, Tim and I decided to build a house, and we sold our first home and moved into a rental home for two years. Tim and I worked really well together. We shared many of the responsibilities within our beauty salon business and our home without fighting or arguing.

I noticed nothing out of the ordinary until my second pregnancy. That was in 2008, the same year we moved into our current home. I was three months along and having complications with the pregnancy.

I noticed a distance between us—our touch and communications were off. I can count on one hand how many times we were sexually intimate during the pregnancy.

Through the duration of my pregnancy, Tim became increasingly busy with his work. My belly was growing, and the end date was near. Our little Charlie was born three weeks early via C-section. In the moments before my surgery, Tim was busy typing on his computer, while the nurse poked me five times to start the IV. I remember looking over at him, tears welling, searching for comfort.

Charlie was born with lung and breathing problems, and they kept him in the nursery for a full twenty-four hours. Because my blood pressure was extremely low, the nurses wouldn't allow me out of bed. Consequently, I was shown only pictures of my little man-cub. Depression crept close. When the doctor finally cleared me to go to Charlie, other family members had already touched, smelled, and kissed his little cheeks—but I was given only five minutes to visit, and then back to bed. When the nurses finally brought Charlie to my room, Tim lay sleeping on the couch. He was so into his work, he even had contractors meeting him outside my hospital room. The first time Addi saw her brother, my mom was there, not Tim.

I didn't recognize my postpartum depression until after it had passed. Neither did I notice how far away my husband was until it was too late.

By the time Charlie was six months old, the cloud of depression had lifted. At the same time, Tim was sharing an office with his business partner, Greg, and they had conversations about the book of Revelation.

Tim's secret was still unknown, but something Greg said slam-dunked my husband into a breaking moment. After that conversation, and unbeknownst to me, Tim began feverishly searching for a Scripture that would allow him to confess his sins to Jesus but not have to be completely honest with me, his wife. This search went on for six months, but in the process gave way to a new man. Tim recommitted his life to Christ, and things on the outside were changing.

I saw more engagement at home when we lay in bed and prayed. I didn't have to prod him to pray—he offered it willingly. We read devotions and experienced true worship together. Our communication consistently improved—we still never yelled or fought; we simply worked out issues. I felt loved. I felt cherished. I trusted our relationship and the patterns we had made over seven years of marriage.

Deleted Conversations

One day, I opened a Facebook message and found deleted threads of conversation not appropriate within a marriage. I felt instant panic. Fear paralyzed me as I recognized what I was reading. *It can't be*, I thought. My gut told me there was more.

Tim later confessed to a ten-year pornography addiction that started back in high school. And then he confessed to extramarital affairs—yes, plural—-that took place during my second pregnancy! My spirit was crushed.

All I had was my faith in Christ—and as I looked to Him to guide me, I had no idea what the next steps toward healing would be, nor did I know how to respond the next time I saw my husband. Even as my world crumbled, I was determined to fight for us, for our marriage, and I refused to allow Satan to turn our marriage into another dismal statistic.

We kept our marriage collapse private until two years after Tim's confession. At that time, our church asked if we would be willing to share our testimonies via video. We did, and the response that followed was incredible. We received notes of encouragement for stepping out and sharing our story. Tim and I were asked to speak at local churches, on radio talk shows, at marriage retreats, and to share our story on national television.

The very thing that made me crawl into a fetal position and cry until I had no more tears, the thing that had offered no hope of repair—God used to bring hope to others in similar situations. I began meeting regularly with women at local coffee shops and through text messages and emails. Long phone calls spent listening, praying with women, and connecting them to the right resources in their area became frequent. And I discovered a common thread running through my communications with hurting women—they felt they had no one to go to in their own church, that there was no group or resource that provided real, tangible advice and support for broken women.

People started asking why I hadn't started yet. When was I going to get a group going? I resisted at first, until a mentor challenged me by lighting a fire under my seat. "Why not?" she urged. "Write your own curriculum. Get it going."

An Ugly Topic

The more I heard about the lack of support for women like me in their local churches, the more frustrated I grew. Some women were told, "Be quiet. It's your fault your husband went elsewhere." Others were told, "Don't say anything to anyone. It's not pornography unless it's in front of a computer." This was appalling! The need to educate and encourage women on their journey toward healing became so evident to me that I had no choice but to act.

God made my future purpose in life very clear to me during the months of healing that followed my discovery of Tim's betrayal. It is now my heart's passion to speak out about my darkest days and to share the hope God offered in my brokenness, during the worst time of my life.

My prayer is that you will see in this thirty-day personal journal the same divine web that held me up when my two feet were too weak to stand and that you will find the same hope I experienced through the cross of Christ. Nothing is too messy or too far gone that God cannot restore. With Him by your side, you can deal with the pain inside and the muck outside. And you can walk with your head held high, offering God all the glory for the amazing reclaimed story of your life.

A Daughter of the King

I am not a professional in the area of marriage and betrayal. I can't offer you *30 Easy Steps to Overcoming the Betrayal Game*. I'm simply a girl with a story who dedicates herself to parenting, keeping the washing machine running, placing edible somethings on our dinner plates . . . and keeping the passion alive in our marriage. I don't have a bunch of letters that follow my name, nor do I have a degree hanging on my wall that qualifies me for this task. I don't claim to have it all together, and certainly there are days when our home would benefit from more structure. I'm weak when it comes to sweets, still struggle with how I view myself, and will be the first to tell you if things are not okay. What I do know is this: I am a daughter of the King who loves me regardless of my weaknesses or strengths. God knew that I was capable of the task to help others, and He has given me a voice to extend hope to lives of women who are shattered from marital infidelity.

My husband cherishes me as his bride and loves me more every day. I trust in us, in who we have become together, and I will stand up for our marriage any day of the week. My faith brought me here today, and my faith will carry me through tomorrow. My hope for you—as a reader, leader, or broken woman—is that you will find how deeply you are loved by your Savior and that you are not alone.

How did God heal me? That's what I am going to share with you. Here are some practical ways you can use *Relaimed*:

1. **This is your story.** I challenge you to keep the focus on your own heart as you answer the "Reclaimed Reflection" and invite God into your journey, understanding you can't change those within your sphere.

2. **Don't rush the process and be overwhelmed.** If it's too much, try answering one reflection and choosing one Scripture to meditate on.

3. **Put your armor on (Ephesians 6:10–18).** You are entering a spiritual battle that the Enemy wants nothing more than for you to fail miserably at as you desire to reclaim truth in your life.

4. **Be in prayer.** Prayer is vital even on a good day. Ask a friend or mentor to be covering you in prayer as you process *Reclaimed*.

5. **Seek God's blessings.** Grab a *Reclaimed Blessing Journal* and write down the ways God is reminding you of his goodness and faithfulness. Journal your prayer requests, and highlight the ways God has responded to your requests. Focus on the beauty of your journey through your own words.

6. **Get connected.** You may feel like you're doing this alone, but it's not God's plan for life to be lived alone. Join the Reclaimed Ministry Community in a closed group on Facebook. If you feel you need to process more, seek out a twelve-week confidential Reclaimed Small Group with other brides seeking healing. You can find out more at www.reclaimedministry.com.

DAY 1

A Cord Broken

The saddest thing about betrayal is that it never comes from your enemies.

—Author Unknown

I tried to take a nap in our bed. The best I could do was curl into a fetal position on the very edge of the bed. I just can't do it. The bed and what it represents to me is too much to bear. It smells like you, fits like you, and—most of all—I roll over, expecting to have the curve of your back to roll into, the strength of your arms around me to put me to sleep, the security of you being there, the feet, the nose noises you make every night, and heavy breathing when it gets too hot in bed. The moments we've shared so many times together are there when I try to crawl into our bed. But your actions have destroyed the security these things have given me for seven years. You've ripped them out from under me, and they no longer live.

From Stephanie's Journal

When words started to spew out of Tim's mouth as he confessed, my body went numb. Even though I knew Jesus was there with me, it wasn't until after his confession that the truth sank in. I felt more isolated and alone than I'd ever felt before. The thoughts racing through my mind overwhelmed me.

I'm going to need to work more hours to afford an apartment because I can't keep this house on my own.

What do I tell my parents and family?

Oh, God, what are my siblings and friends going to think?

How the hell did this happen to me?

I can't ever have Tim see me naked again, much less think about being intimate again.

Where do I even start this process? Is there a process?

Oh, God, he cheated on me. What did I do wrong?

Betrayal is ugly. It's personal and as real as the tears streaming down your face. If you ignore it, it will corrupt your foundation, causing bitterness to tear your life apart. The deception is agonizing. It has no measurement or degree to explain what you're feeling.

I sit with many women and listen to their confession story and hear a common thread—abandonment and addiction. Understanding the "why" behind confession is key to begin healing. When I ask women if they've ever asked their spouse why addiction or pursuit of infidelity is present, most look bewildered. In nearly all situations, the women I've mentored discover a connection of childhood sexual abuse or early addictive behaviors. The disclosure of early childhood molestation isn't known until months into counseling, if ever at all.

For those battling addictions, it's a chemical that has them chasing whatever is easiest to grasp. In our situation, it was the drive of approval for Tim and his desire to pursue, like a hunt. When glancing at pornography left him unsuccessful, he pursued the next best high—one-night stands that began in bars and led to multiple affairs. His addiction to early childhood pornography started out in his teen years but grew into a secret beast that tore away at everything, stealing his integrity and contentment.

The addiction of pornography is a silent killer, as it takes the focus off the bride and places more interest on an image that lasts for mere minutes. For others, alcohol is the addiction that leads to a takeover of all choices and right-minded decisions. Like a lion searching for prey, once he consumes the meal, he begins to look for the next victim to devour.

Knowing the "why" behind addiction doesn't give the wounding spouse a cheap, easy out. It only allows insight into where you need to heal, what the treatment plan should be, and if any specialists are needed. It's important to understand it wasn't you (the victim) who forced the betrayer to choose demoralizing choices.

Betrayal still hurts beyond words, crushing the heart and soul, confusing all your thoughts and making your world spin. The only thing my body was capable of doing in the days that followed Tim's confession was to cry. And it was okay.

I urge you to not allow your pain to determine your tomorrow. God's Word is truth and will bring light to the darkness.

J. Allan Peterson's book, *The Myth of the Greener Grass*, provides a great illustration of how you may be feeling right now. It goes like this:

> A little boy was asked by his father to say grace at the table. While the rest of the family watched, the little guy eyed every dish of food his mother had prepared. After the examination, he bowed his head and honestly prayed, "Lord, I don't like the looks of it, but I thank You for it and I'll eat it anyway. Amen."[1]

Since you've chosen to read this book, my guess is that you've said similar prayers of heartfelt cries that might go something like this:

"Lord, I don't like the looks of my marriage, but I thank You for it. I'll do my best to follow You as I seek healing."

"Lord, I don't like the choices my husband has made and the betrayal he has caused, but I choose to seek You through my pain. I will focus on Your goodness."

"God, I'm not sure how to even talk to You in this moment. I've lost everything. I have nothing to show for those I love. I have nothing to give anymore."

Each of these prayers looks toward Jesus, the Giver of all life, the sustainer of all inadequacies, and the healer of all wounds. We could compare the mess marital betrayal leaves behind to the indiscriminate damage of a tornado that's annihilated everything in its path. The words your spouse launches when he confesses or the details you learn as you discover his infidelity may look and feel like twisted metal from a tornado. It's hard to imagine living through such destruction. When you are at your weakest point, that's when you learn your only viable option is to rely on God.

Ever since Adam and Eve disobeyed God and sin entered our world, betrayal has been a primary delivery mechanism for sin (Genesis 3:6–7). No betrayal looks the same. Some are delivered through gossip or lies. Others through direct action. You may be thinking, *I'll never get over it. What happened to me was so wrong. It hurts so much. I've been scarred so deeply by betrayal and brutality. My anger rages like a nuclear bomb inside me.*

Know you are not alone in these thoughts. The Bible is full of examples of betrayal:

Absalom betrayed his father King David (2 Samuel 15–19).

Judas betrayed Jesus after years of sharing meals, talking, praying, and laughing together (Matthew 26:14–16).

Jesus was betrayed (Matthew 26:69–75; Psalm 41:9; John 13:2).

We read in Isaiah 53:3 that "He was despised and rejected by men, a Man of sorrows, and familiar with suffering." Those closest to Jesus were the ones who'd hurt Him most.

Sometimes physical pain is less hurtful than words spoken against you. I would imagine when the rooster crowed three times, the betrayal Jesus felt is much like the pain a wife experiences in the midst of betrayal.

Jesus knows our pain. There is nothing Jesus doesn't understand, and He is waiting to be your friend in your horrifying darkness.

 Reclaimed REFLECTION

Much like Stephanie's bed, is there something tangible that highlights the betrayal more than any other word or item?

You are not alone in this situation. Does the unfaithfulness in your marriage bring a past experience of betrayal to the surface? If so, do you feel you processed the past enough to not let it affect how you deal with your current brokenness?

Do you feel betrayed by God?

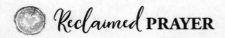 Reclaimed TRUTH

Father, if You are willing, take this cup from Me; yet not My will but Yours be done.
Luke 22:42

Even my close friend, someone I trusted, one who shared my bread, has turned against me.
Psalm 41:9

All my intimate friends detest me; those I love have turned against me.
Job 19:19

Words from a friend can be trusted, but an enemy multiples kisses.
Proverbs 27:6

Reclaimed PRAYER

Father God, I desperately ask You to meet me where I am, as I'm drowning in my tears of pain. I pray my heart would not grow hard toward you and my ears remain open when you speak direction into my life. God, help me to process the betrayal in my life, and walk with me as I navigate to the beginning to begin my healing journey. Thank you for sustaining me through the challenges in my life. Amen.

Confession versus Discovery

A "little lie" is like a "little pregnancy"—it doesn't take long before everyone knows.

—C. S. Lewis

My husband and I should be happily celebrating our twenty-fifty anniversary. On March tenth, I went to send my husband a text, but he'd left his phone at home. When I went to clear my text so his phone would not beep, I saw a message from a number that I was not familiar with. I discovered it was from an escort whom he met online. I checked the rest of the emails on his phone. I counted twelve different women that he had sent messages to.

Hannah

The first night of post-confession, Tim's betrayal weighed heavy on my mind and body. I felt so dirty from the truth of my husband's revelation. He dumped in my lap years of lies with lust, pornography, and multiple affairs. Nothing could remove the betrayal that now seemed to define me.

Many women don't ever experience the complete Judas moment I experienced when Tim sat me down and confessed that fateful evening on April 2, 2009. What started as curiosity, looking at his now-deleted Facebook account, began the discovery of a message that led to a few deleted messages from another female overseas. Messages that disclosed words from phone calls and compliments on new hairstyles. The little I read was enough to make my stomach turn inside out as it sat in my throat, making me want to vomit. I left the screen open for Tim to see what he had tried to hide—and to know that now I could see.

The same night he came to my bedside, desperately trying to explain himself, all I heard was the guilty pleading of his "innocence." The next day we didn't communicate with each other. My gut told me what I so badly wanted to believe wasn't true. As I forced myself to make dinner, Tim walked into the kitchen with torment and anguish on his face and asked me to sit down so we could talk. The moment Tim opened his mouth, the faucet of confession turned on, and it poured freely all over the floor. Not every detail, but certainly all the secrets he'd been keeping buried for over ten years came to the surface. Full confession, followed by intense weeping as he freed himself of the burden he'd been carrying far too long.

I was instantly burdened by his revelation. Many women only get a trickle of information. It's an endless, tiring, pulling, and tugging to pry information from their spouses. This leads to excruciating and emotionally draining months, sometimes years, of attempting to put back together a broken marriage. The withheld secrets fracture any progress to trust the offending spouse again due to secrets still being withheld.

The opposite of a trickle or full-faucet confession is what I refer to as "discovery": When you're folding laundry and find a receipt to a restaurant you never ate at with him. Or a random phone number. Or increased spending habits that lead to insightful investigation into checking accounts that disclose an affair.

I've met with women who have had the "other woman" approach them or—worse yet—received a phone call from the police saying their spouse was picked up for patronizing a prostitute. And for some, they catch their spouse in the act of betrayal. A moment of complete and utter despair.

There is occasionally a subconscious desire for the hidden sin to be found. Tim can attest to this, as the burden of stuffing down such hideous sins makes a sinner spiritually weary. He experienced this in the six months prior to his confession. As he tirelessly searched for any Scripture verse that justified his rededication to Christ but not having to confess all his sins, the enemy viciously attacked him in dreams.

There were nights when a high-pitched shrill came from Tim, followed by slashing around, which would wake me up, only to find Tim physically restrained to the bed with every vein in his throat bulging from attempts to push, lift, and force the shadow off him. Every attempt met with more oppression holding him down in the bed. Once I spoke, the enemy had no power over my husband, leaving Tim physically shaken and exhausted from fighting off the demons threatening him to stay silent. His subconscious desperately wanted to be free, but the physical didn't know how to speak out the confession.

Tim Jackson writes for Our Daily Bread Ministries. In his entry "When a Spouse Is Unfaithful," he writes,

> No words adequately describe the trauma a person suffers when a spouse's affair is exposed. Many report that it is the most dreadful thing they have ever faced—more excruciating than losing a parent, being diagnosed with cancer, or being fired. An affair inflicts a vicious wound to the heart of a faithful spouse. Wounded spouses [often feel], "While I may look the same on the outside, inside I'm hemorrhaging,

and I can't stop it." Most betrayed spouses feel as if they are going crazy—especially during the initial stages of shock. . . .

Gone is the sense of being intact and whole. . . . Self-respect is shattered, and they commonly ask themselves, "Why didn't I speak up earlier when I sensed something was wrong?" . . . Betrayal can strip the heart of any sense of constancy, security, and meaning. Feelings of being used, discarded, and rejected replace feelings of being chosen, special, and valued.[2]

When a husband is caught in a lifestyle of infidelity, it's usually met with resistance and anger. No one likes to be found with his hand in the cookie jar. You're not going to find instant repentance or a changed heart. There have been times when a suspicious wife asks me to sit with her as we investigate phone records or emails until the intuitive feeling is confirmed. All security in the relationship is gone in that moment. The vows you shared together at the altar are deleted and replaced with an emptiness no words can define.

Sometimes confession or discovery can be blunt. Meredith attended the Reclaimed Small Group after being divorced for over twenty years, never to remarry. She shared with me that her understanding of her ex-husband's infidelity came the week after their honeymoon, when he stated he didn't love her. At a later point in their marriage, he asked if he could date another woman. It doesn't get more blunt than that. Blatant betrayal. He used Meredith for his social status and then discarded her like a puppet, damaging her core for decades. It wasn't until she attended the confidential small group that she shared for the first time the pain she'd lived through.

It is imperative to know the "why" behind the confession or discovery. If you don't know what's broken, you don't know what or how to fix the problem. Once you locate the root, the catalyst to the confession, then you can install protective measures to guard against further fatal discovery. This may mean you need to peel back layers, past years—possibly to childhood—to resolve your why.

Your heartbreak is not meant to be experienced alone. Invite a friend or mentor into your life so you don't have to walk this journey by yourself. You deserve to be heard. Your tears have a voice, and God has not removed Himself from your hell on earth.

 ## *Reclaimed* REFLECTION

Are you able to recognize which type of confession or discovery you experienced?

Many women remember every last detail of their husband's confession. The clothes they were wearing, the location, the smells, or other intimate details about the environment. Do you find yourself getting stuck in the details, enmeshed with the confession, or have you been able to move past that moment to seek healing in your journey?

What did you experience post-confession? Name the emotions and feelings you felt immediately after your husband's confession. Reflect on Jesus's presence and how you felt in that moment.

🖤 *Reclaimed* TRUTH

The Lord Himself goes before you and will be with you; He will never leave you or forsake you. Do not be afraid; do not be discouraged.
Deuteronomy 31:8

When they had assembled at Mizpah, they drew water and poured it out before the Lord On that day, they fasted and there they confessed, "We have sinned against the Lord."
1 Samuel 7:6

Then I acknowledged my sin to You and did not cover up my iniquity. I said, "I confess my transgressions to the Lord." And You forgave the guilt of my sin.
Psalm 32:5

I am feeble and utterly crushed; I groan in anguish of heart.
Psalm 38:18

🖤 *Reclaimed* PRAYER

God, I ask that Your Holy Spirit presence would invade my brokenness as I process the confession of my husband's betrayal. My body feels numb—God, move my arms and legs while You whisper gentle confirming words to my heart. I pray that the fruits of the spirit would still remain evident in me, even as I process the horrific acts that have hurt me. Control my reactions, God. I invite You into my mess. Amen.

Pinch Me

Surely the righteous will never be shaken; they will be remembered forever. They will have no fear of bad news; their hearts are steadfast, trusting in the Lord.

Psalm 112:6–7

Betrayal is lonely, terrifying, and extremely painful. I feel isolated. Do people see the torture I'm in? This has sucked the air out of me. The deception and path of sin completely blindsided me—I can't find my footing. I feel paralyzed in my grief. How did I miss all of the signs this was happening in my home? This has destroyed my ability to parent well or to simply see myself as worthy of anything good. Is this really happening to me?

From Stephanie's Journal

If I speak it, I cry. If I think it, I feel relief and hopeful. Strange way to be torn.

Cathy

Think for a moment with me what is was like to see . . .
Lame men walk (see Mark 2:11).

Children healed who were once struck with illness (Mark 1:30–34; John 4:50).

The crowds witnessing Jesus performing one of His many miracles, feeding the five thousand (Mark 6:30–44).

Dead men raised (John 11:38–44).

Peter walking on water with the Lord (see Matthew 14:27–32).

What emotion the guards who went to Jesus's tomb felt when they saw nothing but His burial rags (Matthew 28:4).

The reaction Mary had when she watched her son die a humiliating and excruciating death but then saw her risen Savior standing in front of her with holes in His hands—think what that must have been like (Matthew 28:5–10).

Those lost now saved (Luke 15:1–32).

There had to have been many jaw-dropping and shocking moments in the path of Jesus's miracles and His time on earth. In the same way those who witnessed Jesus's miracles may have been shocked at his healing power, there are also shocking moments that make you want to turn and sprint in the opposite direction. There are situations where truth is heard, but the human instinct is to cover your ears and block with "La la la la la!"

I heard God speak ever so clearly to me in a moment of honest transparency when I wanted to storm out and run, never turning back. As Tim wept in his confession, I turned away from him and looked outside as a feeling of peace washed over me. I felt the Holy Spirit promise me, *It is well.* The room fell silent and a warm rush of peace fell upon me.

I'm not sure I heard anything else, as the secrets Tim had exposed were already too much for one sitting. There was no drizzle, no slow trickle of information that came my way—it was a bucket of burden dumped on me, and the shock left me numb.

Some women never receive full disclosure. My experience came all at once, and my body instantly went into complete shock. I recall clinging to the kitchen sink to keep my balance, not knowing what to do. I felt physically ill, vomit threatening, and my knees ready to give way to physical collapse. Hardly aware of what I was doing, I drove the two minutes to church, and that's when my dam of emotions broke.

If you feel you are not able to function through the shock alone, it is healthy to ask a friend or family member to walk alongside you. My family and a few close girlfriends surrounded me through the initial shock.

There is a period of time when the revelation you received can paralyze you and keep you from making reasonable decisions. Family and friends in the medical field have told me that most patients experience what is called "medical shock" after an accident. This is when organs and tissues of the body do not receive an adequate flow of blood, causing the body to become shaky and the heart rate to increase, and the patient becomes dizzy or faint. The usual treatment is for the patient to sit down and take deep breaths, or they may need oxygen and to be wrapped in a warm blanket.

My guess is you felt some of these same symptoms of shock from the news you received.

In that moment, moving your feet one in front of the other is next to impossible and feels similar to a robot on auto mode. God has not removed Himself from your pain and the earthquake of emotions. He understands your heartache and feels the horror as much as you do. In your darkest moment, God will never leave you.

In His Word, we are told:

It is the LORD Who goes before you. He will be with you; He will not leave you or forsake you. Do not fear or be dismayed. (Deuteronomy 31:8)

When everything around you is collapsing, cling tightly to the promise that God Himself has gone before you to prepare you for the hardships in front of you. I will be the first to tell you, it is not easy to accept the painful truth of betrayal in your marriage. For some it may be that their spouse is unwilling to change or has an unrepentant heart and defensive behavior. You can only control your response and what is in your heart. I encourage you to accept your Abba Father's ability to help you navigate this journey. Choose to be brave even if you don't feel like it, and stretch out your hand in faith.

Reclaimed REFLECTION

Did you experience any physical symptoms after you discovered the betrayal in your marriage?

Was there fear in sharing with those closest to you because of a perceived negative or positive response?

Has your shock worn off? Do you suffer any PTSD from the physical or emotional shock of the betrayal? Some car-accident victims have stated that the smell of twisted metal instantly sets off PTSD alarms from their experience in an accident. Are there any sights or smells that set off alarms resulting in reoccurring shock?

 ## Reclaimed **TRUTH**

Cast all your anxiety on Him because He cares for you.
1 Peter 5:7

Dear friends, do not be surprised at the fiery ordeal that has come on you to test you, as though something strange were happening to you.
1 Peter 4:12

Put on the full armor of God so that you can take your stand against the devil's schemes. For our struggle is not against flesh and blood but against the rulers, against the authorities, against the powers of this dark world, and against the spiritual forces of evil in the Heavenly Realms. Therefore put on the full armor of God so that when the day of evil comes, you may be able to stand your ground, and after you have done everything, to stand.
Ephesians 6:11–13

I have told you these things so that in me you may have peace. In this world you will have trouble, but take heart! I have overcome the world.
John 16:33

Reclaimed **PRAYER**

Jesus, my body is numb from the events that just took place. Give me courage to reach out to trusting friends to protect myself from causing harm to myself or to others. God, I need You to catch me when the shock wears off. Overwhelm my mind, body, and emotions with Your peace and calm so I can make the most appropriate decisions going forward and not have those decisions be rooted in angst or emotion. Cause me to run into Your arms and trust in the wisdom You provide me. Amen.

DAY 4

Emotions Erupting

A time to love and a time to hate, a time for war and a time of peace.
Ecclesiastes 3:8

I'm embarrassed to go to church with the public shame, finger pointing, and judgment coming from church leadership and our friends—the very people I thought I could depend on when the crap hits the fan. I'm so angry at so many people, and I'm scared I'm going to say something or do something I'll regret because my anger currently is driving me to do and think stupid things. I'm furious at friends not seeing the mess unfold and for others not telling me sooner.

My husband's affair has stolen my identity, and I want someone to pay for the undeserved pain I'm experiencing.

God, where are you?

Rhonda

It was three days after Tim moved out when I woke up with a huge chip on my shoulder and was ready to conquer the world. Well, sort of.

My mom was staying with me over the weekend to give a buffer with the kids and to give me some time to spend by myself. Unfortunately, this particular morning, I was ready for change. I decided we needed to make a stop at Target for new bedding, new towels, and a few other things related to the pain of Tim's sin in connection to our home. So with no makeup, hair from here to there, sweatpants two sizes too big, and a turtleneck—I have no idea where that came from, as I don't remember ever owning one—oh, and a sweatshirt so no one would see any part of my skin except my face.

My patient, ever-giving, and humble Mom walked about ten feet behind me as I stormed through the store with purpose. Maybe I forgot to brush my teeth, or she didn't want to be connected to a crazy person overwhelmed with emotion.

It wasn't until I was at the checkout that tears started to flow. I found myself angry and bitter that I had to make these purchases to try and rid our home of things associated with Tim's addiction. I came to my senses before I threw out Tim's computer but not before filters were placed on all our devices to protect what was violated. Tim's affairs didn't happen in our home, but what the marriage bed represented to me was wrapped up in a few sheets and fluffy comforters. It repulsed me to lay in our bed. The prayers spoken, the romance shared, and my anger fueled the reactions and emotions.

Anger is a real emotion that can't be denied. It has to be addressed, or it will manifest itself in destructive ways, whether months or years later. I found myself not wanting to speak to people who either didn't think what happened was a big deal or who minimized the addiction—I viewed them as unsafe to be around. In my anger, I believed they were, in some form, the reason for all the chaos around me—they'd known about the behavior but did nothing to stop it, or they supported the addiction in some way. The jokes people told made me livid. I made a choice to walk away before my words could get me in trouble.

A short time after Tim's confession, Tiger Woods's infidelity filled every news station and sports show. It was obnoxious the way media took his failures and flung them across public television. One day after the news came out, I was giving a family member a haircut. He proceeded to share with me a sexy joke about marriage infidelity. Wrong move, buddy! I came unglued, as the topic affected me personally. To make a joke of it was insensitive and rude.

Anger changes you. You can allow anger to eat at you and destroy the possibility for grace to show itself in your life, or allow the anger to fuel a positive change.

Yes, I was angry Tim allowed the Enemy to easily take over his choices and taint our marriage.

Yes, I was angry at the women who, even with a wedding ring on his finger, accepted Tim's invitation and thought it was "fun" to engage in a one-night stand.

Yes, I was angry Tim betrayed every vow we'd made to each other and to our children. And his pursuit of lust stole intimate moments intended for me.

I was angry I had to experience these feelings and frustrations for days, months, and years as we learned to navigate a new marriage. However, I made a choice to allow the anger to be used in a positive way. My anger fueled a fire to build a stronger us, a better me, and to be aware of the power pornography holds over men and women. It helped me to see the hurting people all around who need grace, forgiveness, and encouragement in a painful fallen world.

I've met with women who, in response to their husbands' betrayal, went out and engaged in an affair so their husbands would know the pain they'd experienced. Others in retaliation choose massive shopping sprees and max out a joint credit card. I know many who allow hate and anger to drive their decisions, resulting in unhappy second marriages, with children being tossed between two bitter people. Anger can destroy you and those around you.

God wants us to take the high road when our character is tested through our suffering, which in turn brings Him glory.

We can choose to react immediately in anger, or seek God's guidance before we respond. God desires for us to walk with humility, grace, and integrity as we face the rage boiling inside. Bring your anger to God before you regret something that is hard to forget or forgive.

One way to release anger is the "empty chair technique" I learned from my counselors. The idea is a "talk therapy exercise" in which you express your thoughts and feelings as if you are speaking to a specific person. You direct your words and gestures at an empty chair, as if that chair contained the person to whom you need to express yourself. This is extremely beneficial in the situation of betrayal, for many reasons. I coach women through this process by having them write letters to ex-husbands or talk to a chair, instead of hurling hateful words at their husbands—this gives the opportunity to release deeply rooted wounds in the pursuit of healing. The freedom many experience through these types of therapy is worth the awkwardness of talking to—sometimes yelling at—an empty chair.

If you are challenged to communicate with the person who hurt you because you don't feel safe emotionally or physically to bring up the topic of infidelity and you fear their reaction, then may I suggest:

1. Find a piece of paper and write what you feel you need to say—with the intent to not send the letter.
2. Practice the empty-chair technique so the anger dwelling within can be set free and the toxic feelings inside can be released.

There were several times I wrote Tim letters with zero intention of sending them to him—this was to flush out all the trash rather than have it fester inside me. I also wrote the women who had walked with him into hotel rooms, as well as letters to myself and letters to God. These were positive steps toward healing, and I felt so much better because I was able to express my anger in a safe and controlled manner.

Every fiber of my soul wanted to tear Tim apart, spit at him, kick him, punch him, and make him pay for the rest of his life—which he'd feared would be my reaction to this newly discovered truth. There were moments when my words pierced to his core, when he'd say, "Ouch, that hurts, but I deserve it." In those times I knew I had to recognize my sin as well.

I pray that as you move forward in your journey of healing—as I still am doing—God will cover you when anger stirs in your heart. I pray as snow covers the ground, making it white, so will his supernatural peace cover your wounds. I pray that He will bind up your wounds and turn the path of anger to one of beauty. God wants to bless, comfort, and give you what you need. Leave the justice part to Him.

Reclaimed REFLECTION

Has anger driven bad decisions in your life? If so, did you gain anything from them?

How has choosing to let God discipline sinful choices, rather than you playing sheriff, allowed you to grow in your faith?

Have you've experienced a cycle of generational sin in your family, and if so, what are you doing to break the anger and betrayal for the next generation?

Anger is explosive. Some women don't feel safe due to the anger brewing in their spouse. Please take this seriously . . . and if you don't feel safe, seek help.

Reclaimed TRUTH

A hot-tempered person stirs up conflict, but the one who is patient calms a quarrel.
Proverbs 15:18

But now you must also rid yourselves of all such things as these: anger, rage, malice, slander, and filthy language from your lips.
Colossians 3:8

Do not be overcome by evil, but overcome evil with good.
Romans 12:21

Whoever is patient has great understanding, but one who is quick-tempered displays folly.
Proverbs 14:29

Reclaimed PRAYER

Jesus, I need you to remove the anger in my life that at times I feel is controlling the outcomes in my relationships. Jesus, help me to cultivate a spirit of peace that will ultimately bring a sense of calm into my life. Control my thoughts and actions and pour your grace over the fires I may have started as an outcome to my rage. I give You permission to quiet my soul. Amen.

DAY 5

Anguished Minds

Each heart knows its own bitterness, and no one else can share its joy.
Proverbs 14:10

I woke up Saturday with a bitter mouth and angry thoughts. I didn't shower, didn't comb my hair or brush my teeth. I was cold to the bone and couldn't even look at food, much less eat anything. Thanks to you, I'm down ten pounds now. Hopefully, I'm skinny enough, because there's not much left of me inside or out.

I feel like you hurled this burden at me and now you're free.

Great. Thanks. I hate this. I hate that you did this. I hate that you cared more about you than your family and wife. The pain goes so deep that my bones hurt.

You make me look and feel like a fool, an idiot, and a piece of trash. I feel nothing inside but the grace of God keeping me going for our children. Was I not good enough in bed? Did I not experiment enough? Not wear enough pretty things for you?

Why have you taken that from me?

From Stephanie's Journal

I craved a physical hug from my husband, and in the same moment the thought of his touch repulsed me and made me angry.

Thinking of what Easter weekend was about had me in deep contemplation. God and I had some all-out wrestling matches in those early hours of my sleepless nights. It came down to this one question: *How can I accept the gift of Christ's cross and not give forgiveness to others?*

Good Friday came, and I knew what God was pressing me to do. Forgive. *Are You kidding me, God? He doesn't deserve it, and I don't feel like giving him a pass.* The bitterness weighed heavily on my heart, and my actions were driven from angry emotions—my lens on life was quickly becoming negative.

Christ leaves no room for bitterness, because He died on the cross to save us from our sins. Big or small. It's all the same to God—but we humans rate our sin and make the "smaller" ones seem like lesser evils compared to the ultimate betrayal of our marriage vows. Bitterness seeps into every area of our life if we choose not to forgive.

Neil T. Anderson says this about forgiveness in his book *The Bondage Breaker*:

> We need to forgive others so Satan cannot take advantage of us (2 Corinthians 2:10–11). We are commanded to get rid of all bitterness in our lives and forgive others as we have been forgiven (Ephesians 4:31–32). . . . Forgiving yourself is accepting the truth that God has already forgiven you in Christ. . . . Forgiveness is not forgetting. . . . Once you choose to forgive someone, then Christ can come and begin to heal you of your hurts. But the healing cannot begin until you first forgive. . . . Forgiveness is mainly a matter of obedience to God. God wants you to be free; there is no other way. . . . Don't wait until you feel like forgiving. You will never get there. Make the hard choice to forgive even if you don't feel like it. Once you choose to forgive, Satan will have lost his power over you in that area, and God's healing touch will be free to move.[1]

I see divorcées of over thirty years still holding on to grudges against their husband's because of unforgiving hearts. Retaliation affairs are executed and ultimately end a marriage. Rifts are created between parents and kids because of ugly fallout that bitterness creates. Friendships are buried because of bitter roots that grow. And marriages are on the edge of collapse because it's just too hard to face the pain and trudge through the murky water of healing.

Sure, it's easy to say it, but to walk out forgiveness and release bitterness is much harder. Bitterness is Satan's deception that robs us of joy.

On that Good Friday evening, my husband and I sat on our living room floor, sharing the elements of communion. I spoke the three words: "I forgive you." I didn't feel any different after I said them. No warm fuzzies, no immediate healing or renewed love toward my husband. The only change was knowing I had given God permission to start healing me from the inside out. The Enemy no longer had any ground to steal what was my greatest gift, joy.

Betrayal and bitterness can cause us to mix the facts with negative opinions. Hollywood portrays affairs like a romantic escape filled with opportunity and success. We can easily allow our minds to create a fantasy of what happened. Society accepts this perspective and places instant blame on the spouse left in shambles. Be aware of the facts so you don't allow your mind to fall into the trap of deceit Satan is wanting you to believe.

Here are some facts I was told:
- "My husband loves another woman."
- "I was duped by lies in my marriage."
- "The betrayal hurts so deeply."
- "This has never happened in my family before."
- "Our marriage has failed."

What I heard were my negative opinions:
- "I'm ugly and not worthy of his love."
- "I will never be able to trust him again."
- "I will never forgive or be healed."
- "Our reputation is destroyed."
- "I'm a terrible wife and mother."

Your entire thought process becomes distorted and inaccurate under stress and turmoil when you allow your interpretation of the facts to take over. Make sure you separate fact from fantasy. I struggled with my negative opinions of the facts listed above and begged God to give me clarity for my wandering thoughts. I often was left with nothing but brokenness. I pressed into Jesus, Who sustained me through the darkest time in my life.

Overcoming these torturous mind battles between truth and fantasy can have lingering consequences. There are days when the weight of carrying the title BETRAYED is too heavy and collapses me. I felt most angry and bitter during what I called my "blue days," when my fear took me captive, instead of seeking healing or listening to God. It hurt too much to face the truth.

Listen to what one broken wife had to say about her anger and how it stole her joy:

My life is not beautiful right now. It is sad and miserable. Filled with hurt and anger. I see no beauty. I don't want to live with someone I am angry with. I pray every day for God to help me forgive him, to release my anger and soften my heart, but I am still angry. I feel as though I will never look at my husband the same. That I will never love him the same, and my heart just breaks. I wish that his affair was emotionless. He abandoned us.

Penny

Part of healing is to be able to see past betrayal and allow it to bond you closer to Jesus. Healing is not a fast-food fix—there is no easy way to heal the pain from a betrayal. God challenges us to "get rid of all bitterness, rage and anger, brawling and slander, along with every form of malice. Be kind and compassionate to one another, forgiving each other, just as in Christ God forgave you" (Ephesians 4:31–32).

I sit with countless women who simply aren't ready to allow Jesus to do this because they are drowning in their bitterness. Again, this is not an easy or delightful situation to walk through, but you must get rid of all bitterness in order to find healing.

Our loving God is waiting to swoop down, gently pick His wounded daughter up into His caring arms, and walk forward with His child as she grieves, adjusts to reality, and processes truth in her heart.

Reclaimed REFLECTION

What joy has Satan robbed you of? How are you going to take back ownership of those things the Enemy has stolen?

How has releasing the bitterness to the cross set you free? How does God redeem you through the process of forgiveness?

Are you more attracted to people in your life who have freedom from their past . . . or do you find it comforting to sit and wallow with them?

Reclaimed TRUTH

Though you have made me see troubles, many and bitter, you will restore my life again; from the depths of the Earth You will again bring me up.
Psalm 71:20

The Spirit then lifted me up and took me away, and I went in bitterness and in the anger of my spirit, with the strong hand of the Lord on me.
Ezekiel 3:14

But if you harbor bitter envy and selfish ambition in your hearts, do not boast about it or deny the truth.
James 3:14

See to it that no one falls short of the grace of God and that no bitter root grows up to cause trouble and defile many.
Hebrews 12:15

Reclaimed PRAYER

God, my heart is turning ugly, stewing in bitterness and rage. I give You permission to show me the areas in my life that need purging. Help me remove all the tainted perspectives, judgments, and attitudes taking residence in my heart. Father God, help me to not portray bitterness to those around me. Give me grace toward myself as I navigate my blind spots, and forgive me for getting in the way of Your will for my life. Amen.

DAY 6

Hell's Duct Tape of Shame

Shames needs three things to grow exponentially in our lives: secrecy, silence and judgement.

—Brené Brown, PhD, LMSW

What's wrong with me? I feel so degraded, and even embarrassed. I must really be an awful, terrible, unattractive woman that he would want to leave me for other people. Why would he want me above all those images he's violated over? The ugly, negative, humiliating feelings bombard me and refuse to stop. Can I be happy again?

Isabel

The water was boiling hot. My body was numb. There wasn't enough soap to wash my skin of the filth, humiliation, and feelings of being violated. By the time I was done rinsing my husband's confession off my body, the shame had scrubbed my skin raw and was now bleeding. I felt raped of everything I knew to be true in our marriage I was overwhelmed and embarrassed because of all the horrifying events. Having to face my new reality and also expose the news to my family was more than I could bear.

The first time back in church, I thought all eyes were staring at me because they had somehow heard of the disgusting truth that was recently revealed. I could hardly stand to look at myself in the mirror because of the disgrace blanketing my soul.

I felt like I was carrying the shame of not only my husband's secret sins but also shame for our kids, families, and friends who were dragged into the mess. It hung on me like an article of clothing, covering me in embarrassment and guilt, silencing me from all God intended. I struggled with self-condemnation for not seeing the root of sin in my husband's life. I wrestled with regret for the movies we watched, places visited, or jokes we shared. It—Tim's confession—radically changed my perspective on how we now had to live with a new normal.

There were days I caught myself glancing at photographs of our family and questioning whether a peek at a pornographic image had happened on that trip or in this place of our home. I'd think, *I wonder if something happened when we were here. When he came home from a business trip, were the gifts given because of guilt?*

As I reviewed our memories, feelings of shame for not protecting my husband at certain vacation spots would overwhelm me—if I'd known Tim's eyes were prone to wander, I wouldn't have suggested the beach for our vacations. Or the opposite—I'd become curious and question the timeline of the addiction, and I'd piece together conversations..

Shame is Satan's way of silencing us. It tells us we're not good enough for Jesus or others, perhaps not even ourselves. Shame caused by betrayal is paralyzing. It strips us of every positive thought, memory, and celebration we share with our spouse. Secrecy and self-judgment create intense disappointment, making us feel unworthy.

Merriam-Webster defines shame like this:

Shame (noun): a feeling of guilt, regret, or sadness that you have because you know you have done something wrong; ability to feel guilt, regret, or embarrassment; dishonor or disgrace.[1]

A 2014 article posted on the website *WIRED* and written by Christian Jarrett states that there is brain research proving shame and humiliation being the most intense human emotions. Otten and Jonas (psychologists) say,

> Shame and humiliation—more than the other emotions studied—leads to a mobilization of more processing power and a greater consumption of mental resources. This supports the idea that humiliation is a particularly intense and demanding negative emotional experience that has far-reaching consequences for individuals and groups alike. The brain seems to be doing more when you're feeling humiliated, but we don't really know what. One possibility, which in fairness they acknowledge, is that humiliation requires more mental processing—not because it's so intense, but because it's a complex social emotion that involves monitoring loss of social status.[2]

It's no wonder we're so exhausted trying to navigate the emotion and burden of betrayal. We need to be aware Satan is using shame and humiliation to render us useless and to pull us away from Jesus, the only solution Who can provide healing.

Brené Brown says in her book *Rising Strong*,

> Many of us will spend our entire lives trying to slog through the shame swampland to get to a place where we can give ourselves permission to both be imperfect and to believe we are enough.

She later goes on to say this:

Scars are easier to talk about than they are to show, with all the remembered feelings laid bare. And rarely do we see wounds that are in the process of healing. I'm not sure if it's because we feel too much shame to let anyone see a process as intimate as overcoming hurt, or if it's because even when we muster the courage to share our still-incomplete healing, people reflexively look away.[3]

There is fear sharing with other people the terrifying nightmare you're living on the lonely journey of shame. Shame carries power in its control over your life. Consciously making a decision to not let shame creep over your wounds and create scars of regret is crucial.

In the book of Genesis, we find the first account of shame when Adam and Eve disobeyed after God explicitly told them they were not to eat from the Tree of Knowledge of Good and Evil in the center of the garden (Genesis 2:17):

> Then the man and his wife heard the sound of the LORD God as He was walking in the Garden in the cool of the day, and they hid from the LORD God among the trees of the Garden. But the LORD God called to the man, "Where are you?"
>
> He answered, "I heard you in the Garden, and I was afraid because I was naked; so I hid." (Genesis 3:8–10)

I imagine my shame was a little like Adam and Eve's once they realized they were naked in front of themselves and God. I can relate to wanting to cover up, to hide, to being ashamed of the situation. There was no fig leaf large enough to cover the shame I felt inside.

Even though the infidelity in our marriage wasn't my choice or my fault, I played a part that led to my husband's decisions by not practicing his love language of physical touch. (I share more about this in in Day 19.) With God's help and daily discipline to silence the Enemy, my shame is wiped clean.

We don't have to own shame. If we have given our lives completely to Jesus, then know this is a lie from the pit of hell that is trying to fiercely control your thoughts and habits. The lie Satan tries to tell us is this: "You're not good enough. You're not worthy enough of love. You don't deserve to be wanted or desired ever again. You are a failure." Recognize the lie, and don't give the Enemy room to spew his venom over your life.

 ## Reclaimed REFLECTION

How has shame come like a thief (John 10:10) within your heart and changed you?

Does shame own you? Do you allow it to dictate your actions, thoughts, and lifestyle?

Is there fear in letting go of the "comforts of shame" versus allowing God to completely heal your wounds? Why?

Reclaimed TRUTH

Instead of your shame, you will receive a double portion; and instead of disgrace, you will rejoice in your inheritance. And so you will inherit a double portion in your land, and everlasting joy will be yours.
Isaiah 61:7

If we confess our sins, He is faithful and just and will forgive us our sins and purify us from all unrighteousness.
1 John 1:9

I sought the LORD, and He answered me; he delivered me from all my fears. Those who look to Him are radiant; their faces are never covered with shame.
Psalm 34:4–5

As Scripture says, "Anyone who believes in Him will never be put to shame."
Romans 10:11

Reclaimed PRAYER

Jesus, show me the ungodly beliefs in my life that have control over my mind and heart attitudes. Cause me to rid myself of any shame the Enemy has placed over my life and to embrace the authority given through the cross. Expose where lies exist, and replace with Your truth. And God, I pray you give me a boldness to speak power into my relationships. I ask with expectation that you silence the Enemy, and I praise you for the victory in my life! Amen.

DAY 7

Liar, Liar, Pants on Fire

Every lie creates distance between relationships.

—Dr. David Powlison

Darryl has accountability [partners] set up, but he was lying and hiding from them too because he was scared of the disappointed reactions. I'm in an awkward space because he finally confessed, but at the same time, he lied to my face multiple times and to his accountability dudes this last year. Can anything he says or does be trusted? I still haven't forgiven him at this point, but I feel I have too much at stake and invested to walk away from it all.

Donna

In the seven years of marriage prior to Tim's confession, I never once sensed a taste of betrayal in our relationship. I never saw residue from the pornography left on the computer in our home. I never had a reason to think there might be infidelity in our marriage. Yes, I'd lied to Tim about the exact date of a purchase or how long I had a new a purse, but never something like violating our marriage bed.

59

Recently, I did a Beth Moore study about secrets.[1] Eventually, any hidden dark secret we bury deep in our soul comes out in a fashion most likely expressed in a negative emotion. There is nothing worse than having someone lie directly to your face when you know the truth is waiting beneath the surface. Realizing Tim had been living with his secret addiction for ten years—and had multiple affairs for the last two years—was earth shattering. It was like an illness had taken over his healthy body, but he never had a diagnosis or treatment, thus creating a slow, lonely death.

Tim had lied to himself for so many years that being able to differentiate between the truth and the lie became impossible. What happened online crossed borders and shared stories with what may have happened in life. Satan is out to kill and destroy, and he did a textbook job enticing Tim to walk far from truth.

Lies are tricky, deceiving you from the furthest thing attached to truth. I experienced this for four years after Tim's confession whenever the discussion of his web of lies was brought up. Yes, I got the full confession years earlier and offered forgiveness, and together we continued to seek healing. The Enemy has a way of muting details that later prove to be true. I wouldn't say the Enemy gave Tim a vision, but rather God revealed "deleted truth" to the mesh of lies and truth happening in Tim's mind. To this point, God has erased most of the images Tim lustfully searched for. He's faded the faces of the women with whom Tim had been intimate, and He mercifully cleansed Tim's mind from the sin that plagued him.

It was in a moment of conversation with me that Tim got a little more clarity and admitted there had been more than just two other women. This is the scheme of a lie, the DNA of deceit, to deliberately and intentionally convey false statements. A fabrication of the truth in his mind created dishonesty in his words and actions.

The scheme of lies Tim grew and nurtured over the course of a decade were carefully crafted by the Enemy, who then clouded Tim's mind from knowing what was fact or fantasy, truth or delusion.

Many couples have said the same, that each spouse has a veil of deception blinding them from the truth. Tim's veil of sin distorted my idea of our marriage from being what I thought to be close to perfect. This made the betrayal all the more painful, and the wound led me to question every shared moment: Was it real or not?

I found myself looking at pictures from vacations and everyday life, questioning whether the emotions captured were real or fake. If the business trips I tagged along with were for his gain or to enjoy intimate dates that produced honest connection, all to satisfy my needs in attempts to cover his. The more I dissected our first seven years of marriage, the more lies I discovered.

I sang this song in Sunday school: "Oh, Be Careful Little Eyes What You See"[2]—a children's song that gives us an example of how to be cautious with our senses. The song goes on saying to be careful what you say with your tongue. As believers, this is a concept we need to address daily. If not, the Enemy will continue to dangle bait in front of us, because the more we hide, the more our hiding makes us weak and keeps us from standing firm in the light of truth. We often tell our kids we would rather have them tell us the truth than to lie to us. This is true in marriage as well—it is harder to hear the truth than create a lifestyle based on lies.

Reclaimed REFLECTION

Do you struggle with the sin of lying? Why?

What is the motivation behind not speaking the truth to others?

Is there something you need to confess to God, to yourself, or to your spouse? What has prevented you from coming clean of the lies in the past?

Reclaimed TRUTH

The LORD detests lying lips, but He delights in people who are trustworthy.
Proverbs 12:22

For there is nothing hidden that will not be disclosed, and nothing concealed that will not be known or brought out into the open.
Luke 8:17

Therefore each of you must put off falsehood and speak truthfully to your neighbor, for we are all members of one body.
Ephesians 4:25

Do not steal. Do not lie. Do not deceive one another.
Leviticus 19:11

 ## Reclaimed PRAYER

Jesus, I need You as my constant voice of truth and reason. Help me to see past the fog of deceit and hear, as hard as it may be, the honest facts of the situation I'm in. Jesus, cause me to see Your truth, and help me to reflect that truth as I speak to others. Convict me of any lies I have spoken to others, and forgive me for hiding in dishonesty. Your Word is life—help me to believe and follow You. Amen.

Heavy Rainfall of Grief

And no one ever told me about the laziness of grief.

—C. S. Lewis

I am pretty sure I am still grieving. How long does that feeling last?
Every word spoken makes my eyes start tearing up.

Shirley

Paralyzed by the events that took place just a few hours earlier,
I sat with my girlfriend who had come to support me as I met with my
pastor. Head pounding with every beat of my heart, my body broke down
with emotion. I was scheduled to work the next day and fully planned
on it, but my girlfriend and pastor knew better. They called each of my
clients, informing them I needed the day off and would contact them
later in the week to reschedule. My body gave way to intense grief that
presented itself as I shed buckets of tears and used boxes of tissue.

My pastor said these words, which have stuck with me for years
after Tim's confession:

You need to grieve for your marriage.
Grieve over what was, what is, and what could be.
You need to grieve over the death of your marriage.

"The death of my marriage." Of everything spoken to me that evening, this statement was the one that clung to me. My marriage had died. My dreams, our ambitions and goals—dead. Those words gave me permission to grieve, and I did just that.

Along with tears came a lack of appetite for weeks. Maybe it was God allowing me to focus solely on my heart and the direction of our marriage. Either way, not eating normally was how I processed and still managed to put my feet on the floor day after day.

After my husband's confession, I spent the next few days grieving. My mom held me as I curled into a fetal position, sobbing over our broken vows. She asked no questions—she just listened, holding me close. The grief weighed me down, prevented me from seeing things clearly, and wore on me in an ugly manner. Mom helped me to bed—which was now the living room couch, not our covenant marriage bed. She stayed there until my tears, many hours later, gave way to sleep. The couch became my home for the next four weeks.

Grief looks different for everyone, and I believe there is no right or wrong way. Some harbor it all inside and never process their emotions. Others wear everything on their emotional sleeves. I read once that tears create wrinkles. Well, shoot! The torrent of tears I shed for my husband's illness and addiction, the betrayal of our marriage bed, and for my own emotions twisted up inside, meant my wrinkles were prone to show up quickly—and yet today I'm proud of every single one! For it was the tears and grief that led to the next step in my journey. Never forget that Jesus wept, and every wrinkle has a story. Never judge someone else for faulty anti-aging cream, since they too may have experienced immense grief like you. "Jesus wept" (John 11:35). God gives us permission to grieve over what we love and have lost.

Tears are okay—it is healthy to let it out rather than bottle everything up inside. Grieve over what is lost and stolen from your relationship. Grieve over the sacred aspect that is ripped from your marriage. Use your emotions to positively propel you forward, instead of what some so often do—stay stuck in the muck. God does allow us to grieve, but he also wants us to find joy in our suffering.

Hurt and anger are also healthy emotions. They reveal you are human. In his book *Desperate Marriages*, about choosing a response to hurt and anger, Gary Chapman writes,

> Hurt and anger are two of the most common emotions upon learning of a spouse's unfaithfulness. These are deep and powerful emotions. In anger, you could pull the trigger and kill the guilty party, or you can turn and walk out the door and never return. One alternative leads to death, the other divorce, but neither deals with the issues that gave rise to the unfaithfulness. And both create another whole set of problems with which you must now deal.
>
> Hurt and anger are healthy emotions. Initially, crying, weeping and sobbing are healthy response to the emotions of hurt and anger. However, the body is limited in how long it can sustain such agony; thus, sessions of weeping must be interspersed with periods of calm. Verbally expressing your hurt and anger to the unfaithful spouse is a healthy way of processing anger.[1]

There are seven commonly known stages to grief. Let me take you inside my grief as it applies to betrayal. This is how I chose to navigate the exhausting process of grief:

1. *Shock and Denial.* With Tim's confession came the theft of my appetite. There was zero desire to eat or drink anything. My stomach did not once beg for food. After two weeks of only sipping water and forcing Gatorade, I was down ten pounds,

with clothes slipping past my hips. I experienced an overall numbness, with no sleep in sight. My body physically tried to deny the truth, and the emotions put my monthly cycle into overdrive.

2. *Pain and Guilt, Disappointment.* The disappointment was thick, like a layer of fog on a misty fall morning. I expressed the initial wave of emotion and thoughts by reading a letter to Tim the day after his truth bomb, in front of our pastor in his office. I spent almost two hours getting ready, perfectly applying my makeup in unconscious attempts to make Tim jealous over what he'd lost. The powder dust of makeup disappeared under tears in a matter of minutes, reading through my journaled thoughts. I continued to journal my thoughts weeks, months, and years later, to rid my mind of the repeating mental triggers, positive or negative.

3. *Anger.* Days into my shock, I decided that a Target shopping trip with my mom and kids in tow would be a good idea. My mom, who was graciously pushing the kids in the shopping cart, walked about ten feet behind me, as she was embarrassed by my behavior. I stormed through the store, charging down the aisles to replace items I'd purged. I was a hot mess. Anger fueled many of my impulsive decisions.

4. *Bargaining.* I call this my purging phase. No one told me about this period of time. I found myself throwing out much of what represented Tim's pornography addiction—underwear, towels, movies, gifts he had purchased for me that possibly were guilt driven, and even our bedding and mattress. No affairs happened in our bed, but his actions tainted our marriage bed nonetheless.

5. *Depression and Sorrow.* After a few months into the journey of healing, I struggled to get on my feet. I experienced profound sadness that eventually landed me in prayer and counseling.

I went on antidepressants for six weeks to help me out of the funk I fell into.

6. *Testing and Reconstruction.* I asked lots of questions trying to assemble the storyboard of lies existing in our relationship. This is not recommended for all women, as some details are too overwhelming and can cause more strife in the relationship. Tim and I also painted our bedroom, redesigning the layout, along with organizing many other things in our home, including our social lives, to best support the process of reconciliation. We watched several marriage podcasts, read books, and attempted to trust again. I parked at this stage for a long time.

7. *Acceptance.* This is where I offered forgiveness, sometimes multiple times a day. I had to accept that his adulterous behavior existed in our marriage, which created a season of lament within me. The pathway of acceptance led my heart to discover a sense of wholeness once again.

Some months later, I felt like I made great progress with my grief. As you grieve, consider your destination. Jesus teaches we will be delivered from evil in all its forms: "He has delivered us from such a deadly peril, and He will deliver us again. On him we have set our hope that he will continue to deliver us" (2 Corinthians 1:10).

Don't skip this critical process and stage in your healing journey, but also don't lose sight of the end. "The end of a matter is better than its beginning, and patience is better than pride" (Ecclesiastes 7:8).

Any upward, forward movement is better than none. I often tell women the moment your movement and faith are flatlined, you're already stuck. As much as it hurts, focusing on one step a day will eventually lead you to be able to walk a mile.

🌀 *Reclaimed* REFLECTION

Do you find it hard to grieve, with bitterness lurking around the corner? Or did God give you the grace to journey through this step with compassion for yourself and others?

Are you aware of your own body language? Grief wears on us physically. Are you able to see the symptoms of grief weigh you down?

Do you build in time for self-care? Do you struggle with depression? If so, are you seeking professional help?

🌀 *Reclaimed* TRUTH

For his anger lasts only a moment, but his favor lasts a lifetime; weeping may remain for a night, but rejoicing comes in the morning.
Psalm 30:5

Though he brings grief, he will show compassion; so great is his unfailing love.
Lamentations 3:32

A time to weep and a time to laugh, a time to mourn and a time to dance.
Ecclesiastes 3:4

Very truly I tell you, you will weep and mourn while the world rejoices; you will grieve, but your grief will turn into joy.
John 16:20

 ## *Reclaimed* PRAYER

God, don't allow me to create callouses over my wounds. I pray I can give myself permission to grieve the things I've lost in my marriage. For all the past areas of pain and torment, I pray I can unpack them and process well. Help me to be still and to know You are here wiping my tears while I deeply grieve my marriage. God, thank You for giving me the promise of joy and causing me to see glimmers of hope that will propel me into a season of rejoicing. Thank You for sustaining me. Amen.

All of Me Is Tired

The moment you stop trying to fix things yourself and acknowledge your need for Jesus is the moment He shows up to give you strength.
—Stephanie Broersma

I'm not sure what I feel right now. I have so many things racing through my mind that it's totally exhausting. Not to mention having to be quick on my feet with answering a four-year-old who is piecing things together. I have so many questions that I want to ask and things that I want to say, but how to say them I'm not sure. I absolutely hate this. I hate that I can't talk to my best friend. I check my email, wishing to see your name . . . and then realize it won't happen. I want to call you to tell you something about the kids, but I don't feel right to do so.

From Stephanie's Journal

Exhaustion makes us do strange and stupid things. I once put a gallon of milk in the cereal cupboard and cereal in the fridge. Obviously, my exhaustion was in charge.

Depression lurked around the corner from sleep deprivation. I spent nearly four weeks on the couch, and having two kids depend on me emotionally so the stress of our marriage wouldn't overwhelm them too was draining. I slowly started to eat and drink again. I attempted a light work schedule, as well as spending many late nights in deep, lengthy conversations with my husband, trying to rebuild trust after he moved back in.

I found Matthew 11:28—"Come to me all who are weary and burdened, and I will give you rest"—refreshing. It gave me the respite I needed for my weak moments during the day. It also helped to have my go-to friends praying to give me the daily energy I needed to make things work. Often my mom and girlfriends called to make sure I had my three essentials each day—put on a bra, brush the fur off my teeth, and slap on some deodorant. If those three essentials were completed, it was a good day!

It's amazing how your thoughts can make you so tired. I found when I sat to reflect on the past, my heart grew tired as well. I thought about situations I may have let slip by and began questioning myself: *How did I not see this? Did I allow all of this pain?* It saddened me that our desire to stay newlyweds had grown old and stale.

In Isaiah it talks about how we will "soar with wings," and I pictured my tired, aching body soaring with perseverance for the race I ran—and still run—to better my marriage and glorify God through our vows. I need to learn to rest in his arms when my body can't take me a thought or step further. Rather than attempting it on my own, I pray I can fly my white flag high and surrender to his protection of rest. I praise Jesus for strengthening my faith in tired moments and for continuing to grow faith muscles.

Reclaimed REFLECTION

Have you had any of those gallon-of-milk moments?

Do you carve out time each day to spend with God?

What are your essentials to a weary day? Do you rely on your faith to get you through, or does your faith need some "working out" so the exhaustion doesn't take over?

Reclaimed TRUTH

Truly my soul finds rest in God; my salvation comes from him.
Psalm 62:1

Consider him who endured such opposition from sinners, so that you will not grow weary and lose heart.
Hebrews 12:3

Let us not become weary in doing good, for at the proper time we will reap a harvest if we do not give up.
Galatians 6:9

But those who hope in the LORD will renew their strength. They will soar on wings like eagles; they will run and not grow weary, they will walk and not be faint.
Isaiah 40:31

Reclaimed PRAYER

God, I'm worn out physically and spiritually. Please breathe life into my lungs and give purpose to my steps. Thank You for giving me a place to rest, and I ask that You continue to draw me into Your presence as I focus on my heart condition, processing the broken parts of my relationship. God, please protect me, as I'm too exhausted to see things as clear as they appear. I thank You for sustaining me and giving me rest. Amen.

Separation/Divorce

God's grace really is enough to carry you when you feel like you can't walk anymore.

—Stephanie Broersma

I'm sick to my stomach and full of anxiety. My husband just texted our son and said he wishes everybody could get along. He wishes to sit me down with his mistress and be okay with this new lifestyle. He must be crazy. He's waiting for some things at his work to settle, then he plans to divorce me. I have zero appetite after reading this, and I'm not sure why my husband feels our son is capable of receiving this information. I don't want this. I still love him. Is that wrong to still love him after twenty-five years of marriage? I feel like I've failed myself, knowing this will permanently end apart from the one I vowed to be with for life.

Elizabeth

I told Tim, minutes after his confession, that he needed to stay home for the kids and not move out, that he needed to be here for them. What an insane thing to think after he told me about all his infidelity! Of everything I was concerned about, keeping the peace within our home seemed at that moment to be the priority. My speech was controlled by my runaway emotions, and my body was going into shock. It was Tim who stated he was prepared for whatever decision I made, knowing his choices carried heavy consequences. I was terrified of the decision that had to be made but knew the Bible gave me permission to exit without judgment.

Never did I imagine having to make a choice to divorce or to stay. To separate or move forward like nothing happened. Counselors don't prepare you for this in premarital counseling. As a happy couple, you don't discuss with your spouse, "Okay, sweetie, when you cheat on me, I'm going to toss your butt to the curb with your bags in tow, then sit and ponder if divorce is the right thing to do. It won't be pleasant. You'll need to find yourself housing and food to cook and also consider how you'll finance both homes and keep the family functioning after your selfish choices." Not your typical cozy couch conversation, by any means.

Recently, I met a sweet wife, Rebecca, crushed by the blow of her husband, Brandon's, second life in another state. This was not his first affair. Decades earlier, he stepped outside the marriage, and they both worked through the confession and the process of healing. It wasn't until her kids went to visit him that they were introduced to "the other woman," forcing this broken wife to file for divorce—something she'd never intended to pursue—because of this second betrayal. The Enemy gripped this man's heart, and he completely separated himself from his family, not flinching as he willingly walked away from them. The fallout is just as destructive, with grown kids stumbling into their own sinful patterns from the lack of fidelity from their father.

I've also recently celebrated with Tom and Megan, a couple who separated for nine months. They finally took steps to move back in together after spending countless hours working on themselves individually before they could focus as a couple again. Both realized if they were going to make the marriage work, they individually needed to heal of past and recent wounds before attempting to reignite their passion for each other. I'm happy to report they have avoided divorce, but not without pain and hard work.

April has been living in a codependent marriage for years, with continued sinful patterns, catching her husband, Owen, in lies. Unfortunately, this pattern has been going on for several years, with the threat of divorce lingering and no action behind the words. The fear of making things awkward for the kids, of people seeing they couldn't make things work, or having the years of lies finally prove to April that they have won—all these troubles have physically paralyzed her from stopping the enabling habits. She allows his behavior to dictate her marriage, and it has won. Like a child without any discipline, Owen has never experienced consequences because no follow-through of consequence has taken place with his unfaithful behavior.

The book *Hope for the Separated*, by Gary Chapman, changed the course of our marriage and how I viewed separation and divorce. Every journey is different. No story is the same, and each couple has a different set of DNA. The decision I made in not choosing divorce worked for us but may not be the right choice for you. Many women are thrown into the cycle of repeating sins, of having a husband who is in the furthest place from repentance.

You may want to remember three things when you are considering these options. First, where is your heart? Second, you are not a doormat. And third, God isn't pleased with unrepentant behavior.

If you are living in an abusive relationship where repeating sins abound, I strongly advise you to seek counsel and find safety. I hate to advise divorce because it's not part of God's perfect design for marriage, but there are some situations where it's best. I high recommend speaking to a pastor and a professional, godly counselor before you begin the process of divorce. I also advise you to have people pray for you and the divorce paperwork.

This process, for many, is as devastating as the initial betrayal confession. The finality of the darkest black in contrast to the brightest white of what each vowed to their spouse can be a torturous time of conflict that sometimes leads to ugly custody and financial battles. Legal separation is no different, aside from a few less papers to fill out at the courthouse. One offers hope maybe things will work out, and the other a door where the keys are lost and the door stays locked for good.

Considering a temporary separation is healthy, and I do often suggest this for the main purpose of giving a couple space to process the confession and betrayal with clear minds. I'm not sure how I would have processed those few weeks of separation in the messy state I was in if Tim had still been in our home, smothering me, wanting to help or getting in the way of my necessary tears. Even after he moved back home, there were plenty of awkward and frustrating moments when he was up in my space, and I simply needed him to back off.

If you remember earlier, we talked about how most men's primary love language is physical touch. If you choose to separate for the benefit of processing what's happened in your marriage and to seek healing, following through with separation on more than one level is important while not sleeping under the same roof. For some men, once their physical needs are met, they stop all forward-moving progress. Sometimes having a sexual separation can be as beneficial as a residential separation. Every journey has its own needs, and with skillful counsel, you can decide what is best for your marriage.

I carefully caution that if you are walking through a divorce and choose to begin dating in this time period, this too could be as great a sin as the one that led to the decision in the first place. Giving God the honor He deserves by waiting until your divorce is final is best. Be honest with yourself. There is false happiness in seeking a new relationship before the other one is finalized. You will create another whole set of struggles and issues by jumping the gun and seeking connection elsewhere. I encourage you to pray through this if you find yourself in this in-between place and in the arms of another man. Think of it this way: you break your leg and need surgery to secure pins and screws to stabilize the bones, and yet the moment the doctor removes the cast, you go out to run a marathon. Good luck!

Please, please, please consider the high risk of injury you may be bringing upon yourself in rushing the waiting period before the next—or even if there is a next—relationship. I'd love to end with some cheery sentiment and a little nugget for you, but there's too much at stake when considering the end of a marriage. I've met some amazing godly women who survived divorce and are thriving. Women who sought God's direction, and He rewarded them with abundant blessings. A journey in which all said God was present in their decision-making and He continues to guide their lives.

Reclaimed REFLECTION

Have you been able to process the idea of a separation or divorce with a clear mind, or have the emotions dictated your actions?

Did you allow yourself space to process after the confession or discovery? List a few blessings God gave you in this time of space and growth.

What was the hardest part of the divorce? Have you been able to pick up the pieces of your life and move forward, or has the finality of the divorce wrecked your world all over again? If yes, you're not alone. Many women state there is a second wave of grief after the paperwork is final. Not because they regret making the decision but because the process and emotions of accepting the marriage is over.

Reclaimed TRUTH

It has been said, "Anyone who divorces his wife must give her a certificate of divorce." But I tell you that anyone who divorces his wife, except for sexual immorality, makes her the victim of adultery, and anyone who marries a divorced woman commits adultery.
Matthew 5:31–32

When Jesus had finished saying these things, He left Galilee and went into the region of Judea to the other side of the Jordan. Large crowds followed Him, and He healed them there. Some Pharisees came to him to test Him. They asked, "Is it lawful for a man to divorce his wife for any and every reason?"

Jesus replied, "Moses permitted you to divorce your wives because your hearts were hard. But it was not this way from the beginning. I tell you that anyone who divorces his wife, except for sexual immorality, and marries another woman commits adultery."

The disciples said to Him, "If this is the situation between a husband and wife, it is better not to marry."
Matthew 19:1–3, 8–10

Reclaimed PRAYER

Jesus, I'm pleading with You to give me the discernment needed to make the right call in my marriage. Encourage me to seek Your guidance and to accept counsel as I choose to separate or get a divorce. Preserve my heart and shelter my family as we potentially steer this road of separation. God, guard my words and remove any bitterness, anger, or tension so that wounds don't get more substantial. Thank You for being here with me. Amen.

Forgiveness

A good marriage is the union of two good forgivers.

—Ruth Bell Graham

Forgiveness finally became the easy part, because I realized (over time) that I could forgive because Christ has forgiven me of all my ugliness. Who was I not to forgive? But the forgetting is the difficult part. The ugly memories try to reappear and control my mind and keep me a prisoner. It just holds me back from the joy God has for me. God continues to help me let go of the hurt and anger, releasing the pain through forgiveness. I realized that forgiving someone doesn't make him right, it makes me free.

Teri

Today I feel the loss of blessings. Blessings that come from a clean and healthy marriage. I think I'm almost ready to forgive, but by no means ready to forget.

From Stephanie's Journal

When my kids get in trouble and need to repent to their injured sibling, I encourage them to say, "Please forgive me for_____ (whatever the transgression)." Most of the time they follow through, but sometimes—especially with the youngest—my request is met with puppy eyes, hugs, and kisses for the hurt sibling, but no acknowledgment of the wrongful action. It seems innocent enough—but there is a progression for a sincere apology that needs to be learned so a child understands the impact of their behavior. When a time-out or spanking is about to occur, the louder the cry of "I'm sorry! I said I was sorry!" can be heard throughout the house. When we follow through as a parent, we help our children learn that there are consequences for bad behavior and it isn't enough to blurt out "I'm sorry."

I wish that we as adults carried the innocence of a child in our hearts. Forgiving each other is a command repeated several times in the New Testament. Forgiveness isn't an option, yet it is one of the hardest instructions to follow. When life races by and we grow older, experiencing more hurt, it seems the consequences are more complicated, and it becomes harder to say the "simple" words "Will you forgive me?"

On Easter weekend as I was about to receive the mercy and sacrificial gift Jesus gave to me, I couldn't honestly embrace Easter without giving Tim the same gift. A week earlier, he genuinely asked, "Will you forgive me?"

I have a choice to forgive as Christ has forgiven me. Would I obey? I knew I couldn't turn back and had to forgive if I wanted to move forward. Forgiving him released the pressure to be mad and bitter and feeling stuck on the journey to healing. The genuine act of forgiveness opened the floodgates of tears that began years of healing.

Jenna is a young woman who told her ex-husband face to face she forgave him for the pain and confusion of his addictions and affairs. He is a nonbeliever and is completely clueless as to what her forgiveness means—for Jenna, she found it to be a gateway of healing and freedom she hadn't experienced yet in her journey.

I listened to Kate, another broken wife, who for years cried daily over the sins of her husband. Devastated, she struggled to let go of the pain and seek forgiveness. "I've gone to counseling, read too much, and continue to struggle in my brokenness, especially when it comes to forgiveness." Every day she reminds herself of the hell she is living in. In a weird way, the rehearsing of her husband's sin gives her comfort, and she isn't ready to get rid of the familiar place she has created for years. She is in a constant state of anguish, and it creates strife between her and her husband. She is punishing herself by not giving her pain to God.

God doesn't wait until we understand what his crucifixion means and the full extent of the gift he offers to us through his death—He gives mercy, He forgives, and He gives life. We need to respond in the same way to others, challenging ourselves to look past the scars and bloody mess so we can offer forgiveness to those who have hurt us the worst. Because God does the same for you and for me, we need to forgive as we have been forgiven.

We can—and should—still hold others accountable for their actions, or lack of actions, in love as Christ did for us. Here are six helpful statements and verses from the Bible surrounding forgiveness.

1. *Forgiveness is not letting the offender off the hook.*
    If your brother sins against you, go and show him his fault, just between the two of you. If he listens to you, you have won your brother over. But if he will not listen, take one or two others along, so that "every matter may be established by the testimony of two or three witnesses." If he refuses to listen to them, tell it to the church; and if he refuses to listen even to the church, treat him as you would a pagan or a tax collector. (Matthew 18:15–17)

2. *Forgiveness is returning to God the right to take care of justice.* It's not our job to punish people for their sins.

   But I tell you that men will have to give account on the day of judgment for every careless word they have spoken. For by your words you will be acquitted, and by your words you will be condemned. (Matthew 12:36–37)

3. *Forgiveness does not mean we have to revert to being the victim.*

   But you, O God, do see trouble and grief; you consider it to take it in hand. The victim commits himself to you; you are the helper of the fatherless. (Psalm 10:14)

4. *Forgiveness is not the same as reconciling.* We can forgive someone even if we never get along with them again. Forgiveness benefits the one offering it more than the one receiving it.

   The next day Moses came upon two Israelites who were fighting. He tried to reconcile them by saying, "Men, you are brothers; why do you want to hurt each other?" (Acts 7:26)

5. *If they don't repent, we still have to forgive.* Even if they never ask, we need to forgive. We should memorize, and repeat over and over, *Forgiveness is about our attitude, not their action.*

   Bear with each other and forgive whatever grievances you may have against one another. Forgive as the Lord forgave you. (Colossians 3:13)

6. *Living with unforgiveness hurts you more than anyone else.* It is like drinking poison yourself but thinking the other person will die.

   Resentment kills a fool, and envy slays the simple. (Job 5:2)

In Old Testament times, when one person sinned against another, it was not sufficient to confess—he had to repay in full plus accept the penalty of one-fifth the value to the person wronged:

The Lord said to Moses, "Say to the Israelites: 'Any man or woman who wrongs another in any way and so is unfaithful to the Lord is guilty and must confess the sin they have committed. They must make full restitution for the wrong they have done, add a fifth of the value to it and give it all to the person they have wronged. But if that person has no close relative to whom restitution can be made for the wrong, the restitution belongs to the Lord and must be given to the priest, along with the ram with which atonement is made for the wrongdoer.'" (Numbers 5:5–8)

One of the hardest people to forgive is myself. I placed an unimaginable penalty no lifetime could repay because I didn't catch the sin that tainted our marriage. It felt like a penalty for not "being enough" for my husband.

Forgiving Tim was often a daily act I had to practice those first few months after his confession. Saying the words out loud or sending him a text to remind him I forgave him helped me when the consequences felt overwhelming. I practiced the same for myself, needing to release myself from judgment and burden. I no longer needed to pay the penalty—Tim no longer needed to pay his.

Forgiveness has finally become the easier part of the journey because I realize Christ forgives my sin and my ugliness in my heart. This doesn't mean it's been all daisies and roses, with sweet kisses and happy wife moments. The journey still presents challenges and triggers. The question remains: Who am I (or who are you) not to forgive?

Forgiving my husband doesn't make him right—it makes me free. Allowing negative thoughts to creep into your mind leaves no room for God's joy to restore you. God continues to help me let go of the hurt and anger, release the pain through forgiveness, clear the resentment, stop the rehearsing of the pain in my mind, and keep me from stewing in my hurt, so I can ultimately be healthy and whole. He promises to do the same for you as you learn to forgive and let go.

Reclaimed REFLECTION

Are there areas in your life where forgiveness is needed?

When you spoke the words "I forgive you," did you experience any magical moment?

Have you forgiven yourself?

Reclaimed TRUTH

Do not judge, and you will not be judged. Do not condemn, and you will not be condemned. Forgive, and you will be forgiven.
Luke 6:37

And when you stand praying, if you hold anything against anyone, forgive him, so that your Father in heaven may forgive you your sins.
Mark 11:25

Therefore confess your sins to each other and pray for each other so that you may be healed. The prayer of a righteous man is powerful and effective.

James 5:16

Reclaimed **PRAYER**

Jesus, I need you. You see my struggle to forgive myself and others. God, convict me of the sin in my own life that prevents communion with you. Break me for what breaks You. Help me to seek forgiveness daily as You have freely given forgiveness to me. Let me not hold onto the past—guide me into the promising future You are waiting to lavish upon my life. I invite You into my desperate need for healing as I release the grip of sin into Your hands. Amen.

Triggers

Be that as it may, I have not been a burden to you. Yet, crafty fellow
that I am,

    I caught you by trickery!

2 Corinthians 12:16

Last night we had a Christmas concert for school, and the "other
woman's" brother sat a few rows behind us, and her sister a few rows
in front of us. It's just so difficult, even though they are completely
innocent in all this. Just seeing them has brought on a new anger and
frustration of just wanting to enjoy a beautiful night without this
constantly tainting everything!

    There are so many reminders of my husband's affair which face me
daily. I take different routes to get places so I don't have to see people.

Mindy

The first Sunday going to church together was nearly comical. As
most women can attest, I felt I had a scarlet letter on my back that stated
all our problems. We looked the part on the outside, with the kids in
new outfits and hair well combed, but on the inside, I was screaming.

Tim had experienced his come-to-Jesus moment six months before he confessed, which had given him ample time to uncover all the filth he'd tried to hide from God. Now, free of secrets and scandals, he was ready to worship. Except for . . .

As Tim was worshipping—hands raised and singing praise to Jesus—I stood by his side (at some distance, of course) wondering who the heck this man was! All the happiness he exuded was the polar opposite of what boiled inside me.

Earlier that morning as we scrambled to get the kids out the door for early service, Tim seemed more concerned that I had my one-on-one time with Jesus. "I appreciate the concern," I firmly reminded my newly reformed husband, "but not everyone does it the same as you. My concern is getting to church. I will read my Bible later." This was all it took to trigger my anger and send me into a tailspin of emotion on our first morning back to church.

Triggers are instant reminders of the hint of betrayal. They are souvenirs of the unfaithfulness once thriving in your marriage. Usually they are highlighted in the first few months or years after the infidelity comes to light, yet they never fully go away. I'm less sensitive to triggers now than during those first few months after Tim's confession.

Being secretive, having body language that something is hidden on a phone or a computer, not being willing to share in a conversation, or the reference to a friendship that encourages negative behavior—all these can send a recovering spouse into a suspicious mental state, wiping clean any steps toward healing.

Triggers can also be physical. Many women can't enjoy a hotel getaway because it reminds them of where her husband brought women to engage in sexual activity. Women report that the intimacy of sexual pleasure is lost because of a husband's fear to emotionally connect with his wife. A particular position sets off memories of being with other women. The Enemy works tirelessly to destroy the joy that comes through restoration.

Listen to Ellie's story:

My trigger is pretty clear that narcissism is the culprit. By Stan putting his best foot forward for a couple weeks, I am now completely set off by the total lack of movement in any direction. I just feel like I am going out of my mind. It may be multiple things. I just can't seem to cope with anything. Stan wants to help and be there for me, and that makes me afraid. I feel like everything sets off my alarms right now.

Like Ellie, who seems blocked by fear because of her husband's narcissism, triggers can interrupt healing if not reined in. Locating the trigger and working through it to the end helps to avoid falling into discouragement and staying there.

There were days I wasn't able to locate the trigger but knew something had set me off, and I would fall into an emotional, depressive state. The only way I knew how to face those days was with worship music and prayer. I would try to open my Bible, regardless if I felt like getting my Jesus on. The most powerful method of trudging through my triggers was to invite Tim into the pain—I'd tell him my mind was lingering in anger or my heart broken with thoughts and images. It was difficult for him to see me struggle, but necessary for my healing.

I warn women to be cautious in sharing their story with other people rather than their spouse. I've had several situations in which a conversation with a stranger, family member, or even a friend has created anguish. The lack of respect toward marriage in general catches me off guard, and it baffles me on how easily women fall into the arms of other men. When your heart is in a broken, vulnerable place, it can be easy to emotionally connect with another man. Yes, there are women who lead Bible studies, work at churches, have an amazing McDreamy husband,

and a home that never has anything out of place, who fall prey to the Enemy and his agenda to destroy their marriage.

An anniversary date of a confession can present itself as a trigger. Anxiety dictates how you act, feel, or speak. When coupled with the emotional anticipation of a confession date, anxiety runs high. It's good to be aware of where your heart is around these dates so you can name the emotion behind the action. Many women say it's like a menstrual period that comes and goes each month. I am not saying we should be celebrating a confession date, but it's helpful to understand how the date plays into our emotions significantly when we pursue healing.

Last summer our family went on vacation to Lake Osoyoos in Eastern Washington. I am a runner, and I was training for a race before our trip. Regardless of being on vacation, I still needed to continue my training. This particular morning, I had to run twelve miles. With my hydration vest secure, headphones in place, and shoes tied tight, I headed out for the long run.

The Eastern Washington landscape is scattered with dry dirt hills that remind me of what Moses might have traveled on for forty days and forty nights in the wilderness. As I was approaching mile seven, my course was slightly downhill on a paved highway. I jumped three feet in the air when I stepped a foot away and saw to the right of my shoe lay a coiled rattlesnake. I sprinted the next mile with the vision of the snake slithering lightning speed toward my ankles. My heart rate shot through the roof, and from that point on, I didn't take my eyes off the road, even when a heat wave threatened to distort my vision. Three more miles down the road, I screamed as another rattlesnake gave me a second heart attack as I made one more impressive hurdle jump. The surprised creature ran off to slither among the grass along the sidewalk.

Triggers are the same as that stupid snake. There is no warning until you hit the perfect crest of a hill on your healing journey. The surrounding landscape camouflages everything lying at your feet ready to bite your ankles and to flow venom into your veins. Triggers can come out of nowhere. The surprise attack reminds us we need to stay alert with our focus on the path, not fearing the triggers. Believe God will make a way for you to use your best hurdle-jumping skills to safety.

Once you know what it was that triggered you, ask yourself how you can avoid it.

Triggers will always be present. Knowing how to deal with them, confront them, and work through them is key to your journey.

Reclaimed REFLECTION

When you are faced with a trigger, how do you respond and communicate your worry with your spouse?

If your marriage ended in divorce, how have you been able to deal with triggers? What are your hot buttons?

If you know what your triggers are, what are you doing to avoid them?

🔘 *Reclaimed* TRUTH

Do not be anxious about anything, but in everything, by prayer and petition, with thanksgiving, present your requests to God.
Philippians 4:6

I sought the Lord, and he answered me; he delivered me from all my fears.
Psalm 34:4

Don't let anyone deceive you in any way, for that day will not come until the rebellion occurs and the man of lawlessness is revealed, the man doomed to destruction.
2 Thessalonians 2:3

So do not fear, for I am with you; do not be dismayed, for I am your God. I will strengthen you and help you; I will uphold you with my righteous right hand.
Isaiah 41:10

🔘 *Reclaimed* PRAYER

God, I ask You to calm my nervous system and bring it back to Your created design of peace. Breathe reconciliation into my body so the triggers and reminders of emotional and physical betrayal can be released. I speak with authority through the blood of Jesus Christ that the Enemy has no grounds, no place of control within my body, mind, or spirit. Cast all negativity far from my life. God, let me seek You when my blood pressure rises, and let me replace the fear with truth, self-control, and kindness. Amen.

A Cord Mended

Trust is a muscle that sometimes has to be worked on daily to build stronger faith in something or someone.

—Stephanie Broersma

I am feeling Satan attacking me in so many areas of my life. I struggle to release everything to God, and not take it back; to rest in God's great love for me, His grace, His mercy, and His promises! It sometimes feel better to hang on to the past because, once I let go, I have to deal with my new reality.

Amy

When the word "trust" is spoken, I immediately think of the childhood hymn I sang in church, "Trust and Obey." It's the story behind the lyrics that make the song so powerful:

In 1887, just following an evangelistic meeting held by Dwight L. Moody, a young man stood to share his story in an after-service testimony meeting. As he was speaking, it became clear to many that he knew little about the Bible or acceptable Christian doctrine. His closing lines, however, spoke volumes to seasoned and new believers alike: "I'm not quite sure, but I'm going to trust, and I'm going to obey."[1]

Daniel Towner was so struck by the power of those simple words that he quickly jotted them down, then delivered them to John Sammis, who developed the lyrics into "Trust and Obey." Towner composed the music, and the song soon became a favorite. It remains popular with hymn singers today.

There are times when I wish I didn't know so much about the affairs and that all the past pain and sorrow I've experienced didn't play such a huge role in the decisions I make today. When the lines of communication and bond of trust are broken, it takes years—or for some, a lifetime—to rebuild the relationship. I usually trust people more than I should. Before our marriage infidelity, I was a trusting person—but when our vows were broken, I lost all faith, and trusting others was challenging.

I grew up in a loving two-parent home where Jesus was evident and a part of our daily lives. I knew to trust in God in the good and the bad. In the past, my trust was challenged in areas of health, death, friendships, and finances. Never could I imagine that the trust in our marriage would snap in two in a matter of minutes. The day Tim confessed, all my faith and trust in him was shattered, and my heart broke into a million pieces.

My "trust muscle" was called into action, and I had no choice, if I was going to make it through, but to fully rely on God to help me with despair, confusion, and the failure of my marriage. I knew to trust and I knew to obey, but it was a long road of relearning how to trust in someone who hurt me so deeply.

I think of Moses standing at the edge of the Red Sea, with an army of angry men set out to kill God's people, who were close behind. As the water rushed as far as the eye could see in front of Moses, God said, "What are you waiting for? Move along!"

The LORD will fight for you; you need only to be still. Then the LORD said to Moses, "Why are you crying out to me? Tell the Israelites to move on." (Exodus 14:14–15)

A gentle promise from God to His people that He will fight—vindicate, make things right for them—but they must move forward. In trusting Moses to lead them, the Israelites had to step forward. They had to move so God could then show them he was for his chosen people and he would take care of them.

Here is what the Bible says about how we can approach trust when it has been broken: "The LORD is my strength and my song; he has become my salvation. He is my God, and I will praise him, my father's God, and I will exalt him" (Exodus 15:2).

The ESV translation reads, "The LORD is my strength and my song."

Regardless of possible betrayal in the future and the pain of devastation from an unfaithful partner, we must at least try to take a small step forward toward trusting again. Staying on the sidelines of the Red Sea only results in bitterness, resentment, and a life full of negative thoughts that seek to consume us with the next rolling wave.

Think about the immense trust Daniel had to have as he was thrown into the lions' den. (Daniel 6)

Job, in all his loss and anguish, never gave up on God and trusted even in his suffering. (Job 42:12–17)

Noah trusted God had a plan when he was given the task of building an ark when rain had never fallen on the earth. God sent a flood and saved Noah and his family. (Genesis 6–9)

Trusting in God looks at a diagnosis of cancer with peace and grace, believing your future is in the hands of Almighty God.

Trusting in God when a loved one suddenly dies and when the pieces to the puzzle of the relationship don't add up right, is a test of faith.

Trusting God after a painful betrayal in your marriage is like standing on a cliff near the Grand Canyon as God says, "I've got this. Trust me. I will protect you, guide you, and give you what you need in this desperate time of suffering and anguish." Getting to the point where you can fall, eyes upward and heart in his hands, knowing all you need is to trust and obey—is so much easier said than done, but necessary for healing.

Trusting God and obeying His Word is to have faith that He will get you to the other side of the Red Sea when the distant shore seems all but blurry. It's one step in front of the other, one step of faith at a time.

When we see from the opposite shore of the Red Sea that God will deliver us safely to the other side, it's easier to trust Him the next time we are faced with a difficult situation. The same goes for our marriage: gaining trust is a process on this journey to complete healing.

Those who hurt us deeply need to be continually transparent, offering information so that the wounded spouse can see and hear that the "need" to go back to the sin is gone. This is not easy when the offending spouse is not repentant. This is not easy when the sin continues and the backlash of life daily whips you in the face. I get that. I often remind women (and myself) to keep it vertical, meaning it's about you and Jesus. Reclaiming your heart back to Christ is the only way you'll come out standing firm on the other end of the shore.

Yes, the goal is to see the relationship heal—but more importantly it's to see your heart find a greater level of love and passion than what was before the confession or discovery.

We both really are ready to start together and have so much hope. After our hellish two days earlier this week, we both look at it now as a gift that was given to us. We have been talking every night for hours after the kids go to bed, and has been the best few nights of our married life—no joke! God showed us how going through those few days, that there can be lots of healing and they only open the door for more healing and intimacy between us. Then on the days when we struggle, I will hold onto these really good days. Trust and obey.

From Stephanie's Journal

Tim did the transparency part well in our story. He offered me password codes and was completely transparent in all the questions I asked of him. He set boundaries at work to protect him, which ultimately help gain my trust in his decisions. He proved to me through his choices of watching movies, choosing dinner locations, or even where he would choose to sit, when traveling, in order to protect his mind and eyes. He allowed me to ask awkward questions, and he answered in order for me to forgive (again) and to hear the progress in his journey.

Ten years later I have more trust in our marriage than I ever did before, simply because he was transparent, accountable, and honest. Trusting Tim again put my heart in an extremely vulnerable place, but the reward has been a restored marriage. I understand you may not have transparency like I experienced, but don't let that stop you from being honest with yourself. God desires your heart to stay focused on him while learning how to trust others.

I stood at the edge of the Red Sea in my brokenness and stuck my toe in the water, and I stood on the edge of the cliff and fell forward, knowing God has and will protect me in my time of need because I trusted and obeyed in His will for my life.

Reclaimed REFLECTION

Have there been situations in your life that cause you to struggle with trusting others and your spouse completely?

Is there transparency in your marriage? Do you hide things from your relationship?

If God threw you in the lions' den, is your faith strong enough to trust in the promise of his word, knowing God is with you?

Trust and Obey

Trust and obey, / For there's no other way / To be happy in Jesus / But to trust and obey.

When we walk with the Lord / In the light of His Word / What a glory He sheds on our way! / While we do His good will, / He abides with us still, / And with all who will trust and obey.

Not a shadow can rise, / Not a cloud in the skies, / But His smile quickly drives it away; / Not a doubt or a fear, / Not a sigh or a tear, / Can abide while we trust and obey.

Not a burden we bear, / Not a sorrow we share, / But our toil He doth richly repay; / Not a grief or a loss, / Not a frown or a cross, / But is blessed if we trust and obey.

But we never can prove / The delights of His love, / Until all on the altar we lay; / For the favor He shows, / And the joy He bestows, / Are for them who will trust and obey.

Then in fellowship sweet / We shall sit at His feet, / Or we'll walk by His side in the way; / What He says, we will do; / Where He sends, we will go / Never fear, only trust and obey.

Trust and obey, / For there's no other way / To be happy in Jesus, / But to trust and obey.[2]

Reclaimed TRUTH

Trust in the LORD with all your heart and lean not on your own understanding.
Proverbs 3:5

But blessed is the man who trusts in the LORD, whose confidence is in him.
Jeremiah 17:7

The king was overjoyed and gave orders to lift Daniel out of the den. And when Daniel was lifted from the den, no wound was found on him, because he had trusted in his God.
Daniel 6:23

Have I not commanded you? Be strong and courageous. Do not be terrified; do not be discouraged, for the LORD your God will be with you wherever you go.
Joshua 1:9

Reclaimed PRAYER

Lord, You know the reasons I struggle trusting others. Show me how to overcome my own obstacles so I can experience more fullness with You. Reveal to me how to become a stronger woman that encourages others to trust me. Give me grace for when I mess up and trust myself first before relying on Your faithfulness. Help me learn how to let others love me again. Amen.

Who Am I?

If you feel unworthy and don't feel you can exercise your authority in Christ, then Satan will work diligently on his assignment, continuing to chisel away at your faith, identity, worth, and perspective on life.
—Stephanie Broersma

I don't recognize me anymore. I find myself doing things to please or attract attention from my husband that I'd never done before. Leo says I'm boring—I feel nothing. I don't even know what I want for me. I don't know what brings me joy now. I feel like I'm going crazy. It's hard . . . because I feel so ugly and broken. For ten years I have spent every ounce of energy trying to save my marriage, that I haven't been able to take care of me.

Betty

Growing up, I always had a vision of what I thought my life should look like. I was pursuing three potential job careers and landed in the hair business. After two years of working at a local salon, my husband came home informing me we were buying a salon. What? When we bought the new business, I missed the gals at the old salon and the ease of working without the chaos of remodeling, hiring, firing, and managing a business of our own.

Don't get me wrong—we, a handful of young stylists, had a fantastic time working together as team in the new salon. But at the same time Tim and I purchased the business, my husband was more focused at his work. We both worked crazy long hours—sometimes sixty-plus hours a week. We hardly shared a meal at home.

And life was about to get busier.

Our firstborn, Addison, came two years after the purchase of the salon. Plus, traveling with Tim's musical quartet was at its height, taking us as a family to many different states and countries. It wasn't until our son Charlie was born that things became more complicated. Throughout my second pregnancy, Tim and I had lost physical touch with each other, and the complications with the pregnancy had left me empty. Then there was the battle of emotions when my sister Traci was diagnosed with cancer. My life kept changing rapidly, moving faster and faster. Without understanding the entire picture, depression set in.

Then one day, because of financial reasons, we chose to sell the salon. It had been my life, my project, and my passion for five years. It had in some ways become part of my identity. Instantly, I became a stay-at-home mommy with a small salon in our home. On the horizon, as our children grew, there was the prospect of homeschooling. I had hobbies, but time didn't allow much of anything else as I sacrificed my time in exchange for Tim's pursuits.

The majority of women who walk through betrayal express how devastated their self-image is after picking up the shattered pieces of their marriage. This was the most challenging consequence for me because of the sin resulting from Tim's confession. I felt there was no competing against the air-brushed images of pornography.

For many women, struggling with the residue of betrayal over a husband's engagement with pornography hurts worse than the knowledge of physical affairs. With every glance at pornography, Tim took that look away from me, the intimacy stolen and placed on a temporary fix. The affairs were a result of the addiction gaining momentum.

Seven years into the marriage, I lost who I was and the person I thought I married. Weeks after Tim shared his struggles, he met with a guy named Frank, who also wrestled with addiction. At first Tim wasn't sure about the connection, but in the end, because of his conversations with Frank, Tim painfully came to grips with his selfish addictions and how they stole my identity. At one point during his addictive behaviors, he'd told me he was no longer attracted to his empty shell of a wife. I'd given up all of my dreams to support his hobbies, and in return it destroyed me and felt I lost my identity.

It took me a long time and counsel to renew my identity in Christ. I knew I was a daughter of the King, but when my marriage went off track, I realized how empty I had become. I had no passion or hobbies. I lost friendships and felt depleted of everything I had worked for in the past. It went beyond the surface of "I'm a mommy and a wife." I was having an identity crisis because of the pain in our marriage. After Tim confessed, going to church together was also emotionally confusing for me. We sat next to each other, lived in the same house, and shared life together. Who was he?

That first Sunday, I collapsed in our bed and sobbed for fear of who I was and confusion about this new person I was married to! God took my broken, beat-up husband and made him new. I watched in wonder but tried to figure out where I fit in his restored life.

I recently read an anonymous online study about identity in Christ. I love how the writer condensed a description of this identity into a paragraph:

When we don't realize who we are in Christ, our faith will be crippled. If you don't feel worthy to exercise your authority in Christ, then you won't be doing it in the fullness of faith and will lack assurance. The truth is that we, by our own power and effort, are unworthy—but it is the Blood of Christ that makes us worthy. And if we say we are unworthy when the Blood says we are, then we are denying the work that Christ did for us on the cross![1]

It is critical to know who you are in Christ as you offer yourself in marriage. Husbands and wives need to have individual relationships with their risen Savior and then together share a Christlike union. If not, you will find yourself drained and depleted of everything.

Being able to stand strong in God's presence, understanding his character and your identity, is an important aspect of a marriage. Over the years, I have been able to rediscover who I am and continue to build my character in Christ. My identity isn't defined in the sins of the past or from the mistakes in my marriage. My identity is found in the risen Savior.

Reclaimed REFLECTION

If you had to write on a notecard attributes about yourself, what would they be? Would they look different if you had your spouse write them, or a close friend write them?

Where or what do you find your identity to be rooted in?

What evidence is there that Christ is working in your life?

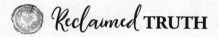 *Reclaimed* **TRUTH**

But you are a chosen people, a royal priesthood, a holy nation, a people belonging to God, that you may declare the praises of him who called you out of darkness into his wonderful light.
1 Peter 2:9

Yet to all who received him, to those who believed in his name, he gave the right to become children of God.
John 1:12

I am the vine; you are the branches. If a man remains in me and I in him, he will bear much fruit; apart from me you can do nothing.
John 15:5

But our citizenship is in heaven. And we eagerly await a Savior from there, the Lord Jesus Christ.
Philippians 3:20

Reclaimed **PRAYER**

God, thank You for loving me exactly as I am. With Your help, show me the ungodly beliefs I'm living in and eradicate them from my hard drive as the lies have shattered my view of myself. Silence the Enemy's mouth; cause him to be as far from my life as possible as I find a new identity in this journey. Speak Your truth to my inner core, and cause me to walk in confidence that I am a child of God. Bring people in to encourage me in this search of who I am. Push me into praise all throughout the day. Amen.

First Words

The most unfortunate form of communication is a misunderstanding or lack of words. If there is any hope for us, we need to communicate.
—Stephanie Broersma

I thought about our communications skills on my walk tonight. For so long, I thought you were just not in the talking mood or exhausted from work. I've wanted for so long to be able to talk to you about so many random things. To have a conversation without any end in sight. I started to think I didn't have anything good to say because I got nothing back in response. Looking back over the past seven years with the recent discovery has shed light on why you never wanted to have certain conversations: it would lead to the truth being exposed. And for that, I hate you. I hate that the sin in your life stole that joy from your wife. I'm confused and exhausted with headaches from all the thoughts filtering through my mind. I have questions but I'm not sure I can handle the answers.

From Stephanie's Journal

As a parent of a two-year-old, communication between my daughter and me is in the form of hand motions, constant repeating, and guessing at the meaning of the foreign language that comes out of her mouth. I can usually tell what our daughter is trying to say, because I'm with her most all the time. I can see it in her expression how she's feeling or know by her cry what she needs. As with all four of our children, I am able to hear in their cry what they need from me as their mother.

In marriage, I believe it is the same. Spouses can tell by body language, tone of voice, or lack of conversation how the other person is feeling. Communication is key to any successful marriage and often is read through body language.

I believe one of the reasons our marriage fell apart is because of the lack of communication. We said what the other wanted to hear and knew if we were to really speak truth from our hearts, things might get ugly.

Growing up, I witnessed others stuffing down their pain and emotions rather than discussing them. I hate confrontation, so sometimes it's easier to be silent than to speak—a witnessed behavior I started practicing myself. I became codependent, a person who lived to please others, never finding my own voice or feeling my opinions were heard.

I had no reason to confront the unknown secret sin that consumed our marriage, because I saw no evidence except my husband growing further from me. I thought it was busyness with work and home life. Little did I know what was really going on.

Tim's confession forced us to communicate. At first I journaled my innermost thoughts and hurts, and then I found the strength to share them with my husband. I was able to express to him what was in my heart more clearly than ever before. My fear didn't stop my tongue, and my words were spoken in love.

The day after my husband's confession, we met with our pastor. I read aloud a letter to Tim expressing my vulnerable heart with nowhere to hide from all I was feeling. Ten years later, I can still express my concern in love, while holding my husband accountable, as I ask, "How are your eyes? How is your mind?" This style of vulnerability has been key to our constant revival of how we communicate with each other. It's not accusatory, nor does it spew hatred toward the other person—it's simply protecting what we've worked so hard to restore.

Being transparent in communication and finding new ways to express your love toward each other will not only build trust but strengthen your vows. Gary Chapman in his book *The Five Love Languages* helps us discover what our love language is and how vital it is to speak each other's language in a marriage. This has made a world of difference in the way we communicate, and it also provides accountability to have our spouse's best interest at heart.

If you are separated or divorced, this still applies. Whether it's organizing custody plans or scheduling kids' activities, you still need to work hard on communicating in love. Pursuing a reclaimed and whole heart refers to all areas of our lives, including the times when you may have to deal with the one who hurt you.

I often get desperate texts from hurting women begging for advice or a simple word of encouragement. This particular text came from Tessa, a woman trying to make her marriage work after her husband had multiple affairs. She is living in a verbally abusive relationship with a husband who will not own his part in the current mess. Together, they are seeking counseling as individuals and as a couple to work on the core issues at hand.

This is what Tessa said after a few months post-discovery:

I keep the hope, but then one hour (or even minutes) I'm super excited and feel freedom, and the next anxious about what's to come and how to overcome this. It's exhausting. I'm trying to figure out how to effectively communicate what I'm feeling and trying to figure out what it is exactly that I am going to need from Greg from here on out for reassurance and building back trust.

Defensiveness was the theme of counseling today. In some strange way, though, that was progress.

Effective communication can be achieved with your tone of voice, body language, and ability to speak in love. The reward results in finding new levels of intimacy in your relationship. Sometimes that means going outside your comfort zone and having to discuss what you're really thinking. Trust me, the more honest you can be will help your husband think about his need to open up and share his thoughts. If you were never taught to communicate well, this will take some practice. Don't get discouraged!

Something to consider when you are reengaging in communication is understanding how you respond in conversation. There are four common responses that can ruin your relationship and prevent you from hearing your spouse correctly. Knowing which is your most common coping mechanism when you are feeling fearful, insecure, or threatened will help you understand why you respond in certain ways and even why your spouse reacts the way he does.

Flight—You find yourself busy with distractions: sleeping, hyperactivity, activities; never home; binging on Netflix.

Fight—You attack others when you feel fearful. You intimidate other people, and you have unreasonable demands to control the situation.

Freeze—You give up, blank out, feel stuck, and hold your breath in dread.

Fawn—You tend to be a people pleaser, constantly walking on eggshells. You rarely show the real you because you fear you may later regret it, and the purpose for your talk is lost because your emotions run your mouth.

I'm still working on not relying on my codependency to please others. The "innocent fawn" response was my go-to prior to Tim's confession.

My opinion and words do matter. My thoughts do have a place to be shared in safety and confidence. Now, when I hold on to my thoughts or emotions, Tim is quick to call them out because he knows my body language enough to see I have something I need to get off my chest. He'll often say, "Where is my wife?" We share painful conversations when needed, and I have no fear in asking the potentially painful question as it relates to my healing. We are still a work in progress, but I believe we will be until the other side of heaven.

Are you a woman who is currently separated from her spouse? How do you communicate? It is sometimes best to communicate via email or text so it is documented if there ever comes a time when you need to protect yourself and your kids and have to present evidence to a judge. Many women find this a much healthier form of communication with their separated spouse because they don't feel like they are being cornered into a form of speech that is unproductive. For example, if the marriage is hostile, having to verbally speak to your spouse could set off alarms and triggers resulting in raised voices and you possibly regretting later what was said. Face-to-face conversation is always best and should be the primary form of communication before text, email, or Facebook messaging. You miss the body language and tone of voice when hiding behind devices.

If a third party is needed to communicate in a healthy manner, please don't hesitate to ask a mentor, pastor, family member, or friend to sit and listen. The conversation has to begin somewhere. The first time will be emotionally charged and driven, but know that expressing your emotions is not wrong. Many of my conversations with Tim were heard through tears and not words.

Talking to Jesus is safe and brings comfort. If you are unsure where to begin, start there.

Reclaimed **REFLECTION**

How is your coping mechanism affecting your marriage or other relationships? Have you witnessed others' body language creating an awkward situation?

If your marriage ended in divorce, how do you communicate with others about your ex-husband? Do you portray hatred in your words around your kids?

In today's world, we often converse with each other through text or email. Do you see yourself hiding behind a text when forced to have a challenging conversation? If so, why?

Reclaimed **TRUTH**

My dear brothers, take note of this: Everyone should be quick to listen, slow to speak and slow to become angry.
James 1:19

In my distress I called to the LORD; I cried to my God for help. From his temple he heard my voice; my cry came before him, into his ears.
Psalm 18:6

A gentle answer turns away wrath, but a harsh word stirs up anger.
Proverbs 15:1

Reckless words pierce like a sword, but the tongue of the wise brings healing.
Proverbs 12:18

Communication Challenge

Try for a week to put your device down and text less, write a friend a letter, or pick up the phone to actually speak to another soul. Be aware of what and how you are communicating your words to others. Take note of what triggers panic, harsh words, or codependent tendencies.

For many, the first conversation that needs to happen is between you and God. It starts with this: "Hey, God, I'm so broken. I don't even know where to start."

Reclaimed PRAYER

God, You hear the words in my heart and those racing through my mind. Help me to articulate what is stirring inside me and find the strength to speak up when my voice needs to be heard. Challenge me to walk out with grace and humility as I share my heart with those I love. Open my ears to hear what others are telling me, and give me discernment for the advice given. Let people hear Your love as I speak. Amen.

Relearning the ABCs of Marriage

Time is your most precious gift because you only have a set amount of it. You can make more money, but you can't make more time.

—Rick Warren

Learning about my own "why" is just as tiring as to the "why" Kevin seeks others rather than me. I started working out again last night and tried to overload my system with endorphins, as I can finally see the depression aspect of all this. Grateful for God's gentle insight in showing me how long ago these barriers were placed in my heart.

Lexie

I've never enjoyed studying and always struggled through school, especially with math. Are you really going to use all this X equals Y and Z nonsense in real life anyway? I admire those who can read a book, memorize important facts, and shortly after, ace a test. Never in my childhood did I desire to go to a four-year college, though I had dreams of becoming a teacher, a social worker, or a hairstylist, while managing being a wife and mom.

After owning my hair salon for a few years, my hair started to turn gray as I endlessly spent my days fixing self-inflicted haircuts on adults and children. My dream of becoming a teacher took the form of homeschool for seven years. Visions of becoming a social worker came in the form of refereeing arguments between our kids and maneuvering through anxiety disorders, ADHD, and sensory issues while filling out paperwork for our youngest daughter's adoption.

God gave it all to me minus a college degree plaque on the wall. Instead, I had a bookshelf full of related topics and the Bible as my guide.

When active in the salon, I tracked trending hairstyles to give my clients the latest looks. As a homeschool mom, I followed state guidelines and made sure I taught the best to my kids. I see young parents with academic degrees, and they can't use them anywhere. It's certainly a great thing to educate yourself—you have to be motivated to study for a degree in order to become the best in your career. But there is an end goal when pursuing a degree, and relationships should have a goal as well.

Today, marriages lack understanding when it comes to the need for "continuing relationship education." Couples get their "degree"—the exchange of "I dos"—and relish the newlywed state for a few years, sometimes less. Then life happens. Children appear, and jobs take priority, with daily routines mixed in with household chores and adventures that include digging toys out that are tossed down the drain. How is it we put thousands of dollars of value on a piece of paper to gain a career but we don't think about investing in our marriages with the same intensity?

It happens slowly, and we don't see it coming. Married life becomes something like two college roommates passing in the hall.

Acting on marriage vows needs to include continuing education to learn all we can about our relationship, and this education should be at the top of the to-do list. Sometimes we make it too complicated. A simple daily devotional, attending a marriage conference, or listening to a marriage podcast, DVD, or online study can turn a dull marriage into something beautiful.

Consider this your daily vitamin for your marriage, or any relationship, for that matter. A healthy pursuit to engage with one another encourages the relationship to flourish.

The first few months after Tim and I separated, we devoted our time together to learn about our marriage and develop our individual relationships with Christ. We were then able to minister to one another. We listened to podcasts, participated in marriage seminars, read an entire bookstore worth of books, and prayed continually. We even started dating each other again. We couldn't forget our history, but we understood our relationship needed to start fresh.

Our first few dates were at the coffee shop, and it was awkward staring at each other as our coffee turned cold. Then the dates switched to dining out, and eventually an evening stroll along the waterfront. The dates tended to go okay—until, on a drive home after another lukewarm evening out, I ruined all progress by asking for intimate details about the affairs. My timing was a wee bit off on that one, but it was all part of my progress, part of what I needed. Tim—although not wanting to answer—understood. He owned the consequence of our awkward conversations and humbly gave me what I needed to know.

Understanding the grip the Enemy has over our minds and everyday life is crucial to protecting our marriages. Covenant Eyes is an internet accountability and filtering program that states these facts about the suffocating addiction of pornography:

- 5% of pastors do not make themselves accountable to anyone.[1]
- 7% of pastors said viewing pornography was a "current struggle."[1]
- 1 million daily average visits to Pornhub, the world's most popular porn website.[2]

- 20 billion annually is profited/generated globally from the pornography industry.[3]
- 1 in 5 mobile searches are for pornography.[4]

I was naïve to these statistics and still don't want to believe they are true. The addiction of pornography is powerful and plays a role in most affairs. When men are tempted with lust, their first look is automatic and purely biological; the second look becomes a choice, unless there is intent to seek out lust in the first place.

Understanding how God created our bodies has me in awe, and I ponder how the heck He did that in a day. God gave Adam and Eve a pure bond as husband and wife, designing the sexual part of marriage to be for their eyes only. The destruction of marital intimacy happens when we allow outside images to destroy the expectation of pleasure that is meant to be kept within the boundary of marriage.

Part of the safeguard against these vicious attacks on our marriage was to install what I call "firewalls." Like a computer firewall, firewalls in our marriages guard against "viruses" that mess with our thought processes. I had to pull my head out of the ground and see how the Enemy was invading my home! This is something I never want to be ignorant of again—especially with our children growing into adults and eventually entering into their own relationships.

Part of ministering to my husband is understanding how to protect him and the ways the Enemy and deceiver attack him best. Once my eyes were open to the accessible forms of pornography, I was astonished and disgusted how easily society allows this perversion and the extreme levels it is accepted. I became more aware of how I dressed to not allow another to stumble, out of respect for my husband and myself.

At church I become angry when watching women walk into a holy place in a slinky Friday-night club outfit. My heart sinks for my husband and all the other men struggling to bounce their eyeballs around in an effort to not land on peek-a-boo shorts or skirts and low-cut tops revealing breasts.

I toss in the trash all the junk mail and magazines. We installed online apps to screen our TV shows and movies. (What's concerning is how others who aren't directly impacted by the consequences of pornography don't seem to notice the protection others must place in their lives.)

Like studying toward a master's degree, I educated myself on our relationship and the safeguards necessary to protect us, and I encourage you to learn all you can about your relationship. The first is to learn about yourself. Second, learn about your husband, and diligently pray for him. Third, learn how God intends for both of you to coexist as man and wife. Do yourself a favor and pour energy into expanding your knowledge about how your marriage can thrive.

Reclaimed REFLECTION

Is there a lack of learning about your relationship within your marriage? Are you intimidated by marriage conferences? Why?

What are some ways you have grown deeper in your marriage?

When was the last time you asked your spouse, "What is your favorite _____ (fill in the blank: color, meal, sport, hobby, vacation, memory, etc.)?" How well do you know each other?

Reclaimed TRUTH

Let the wise listen and add to their learning, and let the discerning get guidance.
Proverbs 1:5

Instruct a wise man and he will be wiser still; teach a righteous man and he will add to his learning.
Proverbs 9:9

The heart of the discerning acquires knowledge; the ears of the wise seek it out.
Proverbs 18:15

For the word of God is living and active. Sharper than any double-edged sword, it penetrates even to dividing soul and spirit, joints and marrow; it judges the thoughts and attitudes of the heart.
Hebrews 4:12

Reclaimed PRAYER

God, you hear the words in my heart and those racing through my mind. Help me to articulate what is stirring inside me and to find the strength to speak up when my voice needs to be heard. Challenge me to walk out with grace and humility as I share my heart with those I love. Open my ears to hear what others are telling me, and give me discernment for the advice given. Let people hear Your love as I speak. Amen.

New Beginnings of Hope

To love means loving the unlovable. To forgive means pardoning the unpardonable. Faith means believing the unbelievable. Hope means hoping when everything seems hopeless.

—G. K. Chesterton

Once in a while I get the feeling that things are getting back to normal, and then I get hit with an overwhelming sadness and realization that what has happened is truly the shits! It's a constant intentional trusting that God's promises and strength are more powerful than the pain.

Ellen

I wish hope could be found as easily as dust bunnies under furniture. Some days it feels like you need to tear down the walls of Jericho[1] in order to see a glimmer of hope. Other days hope shines through brightly, like a clear sunny afternoon. It's in the moments where the sun is shining that you feel there is progress and can see some hope. However, you also see the dirt and smudges from the stress of life too.

Hope is a verb and not an emotion. We have to actively work on seeing the best in our situations, to see God in the little details as He weaves everything together for His purpose and plan. It's our emotions that derail us from progress, much like the dirt and smudges on windows, which make our vision cloudy and blurry. God wants us to see not the blurriness but the rays shining through.

In an attempt to find some truth and something tangible to read to give me direction and hope, I visited the local bookstore days after my personal bomb detonated. As I lived, breathed, and fueled myself in God's Word, I wanted to gain more knowledge to make the best decisions moving ahead. I ended up with a stack of books ten high. One book on top clearly stated the purpose for my reading content. It was unfortunate the cashier didn't read the title before asking how I was doing. Oops. I'd thought the title *After the Affair* would be a clear indication I was hanging by a thread. If the title of the book hadn't given me away, the lack of care for my appearance should have. I must have looked so disheveled with no makeup, hair winging every direction, and eyes so puffy they looked like whipped frosting. I left feeling angry that I had to spend money on these books and that I had to educate myself on this topic.

Thankfully, it was the first book I opened that changed my entire course in our story. *Hope for the Separated*, by Gary Chapman, was the book that spun a one-eighty turn on my thought process. For our entire marriage I'd always said, "No second chances. I will never stand up to that behavior." As a hairstylist, I had countless women divulge their marital distress, and then some, while sitting in my salon chair for two hours with my full attention. I often say I earned a counseling degree from all the free sessions I gave at the salon. At one time, I was the stylist for both a husband and wife in distress, as well as the husband's mistress and the wife's new boyfriend. They don't train you for that at cosmetology school!

One client was a nurse, and a few weeks earlier, she'd had a patient come in for her yearly physical. When my client got the patient's test results back, she called the woman into the office to discuss the results. The test revealed she was positive for HPV. With shock and confusion, she called her husband, perplexed as to how this could happen. Sadly, this was the way she'd learned of her husband's yearlong affair. His selfish desire led to this innocent wife receiving news of having contracted a sexually transmitted disease because of her husband's infidelity.

Later, Tim was surprised when I firmly stated if I ever found out I had contracted a disease from an affair, there would be no second chances. Poor guy had no warning I would come home with this type of conversation, but little did I know then that I would reflect back to that numerous times. The first night after Tim's confession, I vividly remembered that "no second chance" conversation and became angry that it had meant nothing to Tim. I'd warned. He'd known what was at stake.

Hope was nowhere to be found in those empty, sleepless nights. At that point I didn't even know what to hope for. But God had ideas to soften my heart and strengthen my faith. I felt depleted of all emotion, like an empty watering can. I felt bad for having negative thoughts and told myself I still loved him. But how could I love the person who shattered my heart? I viewed Tim's absence in our home during our separation as lack of progress, but that's exactly where God wanted me as He broke me of my negative thinking pattern and filled me with the idea that there was hope for my future.

I found myself unable to set down Chapman's book, and when I couldn't find rest, I picked up the book and reread chapter after chapter. I leaned in and gave God permission to fill my spirit with hope, highlighting nearly every word that spoke to me. After weeks on the couch, I gained the strength to sleep in our bed—alone. Once Tim moved back home, he slept on the floor by the couch until eventually I invited him back to the bedroom. That gave me hope of things to come—the first night falling asleep with our toes touching and hands holding. Laughs shared and even the rebirth of cuddling! We started dating again, simple coffee shop dates—they were a glimmer of hope for a rekindled marriage. Not to say there weren't also clunky, awkward moments. We took little baby steps to put our fractured marriage back together.

I learned quickly that this was my journey I had to walk through. Tim had his own journey, and together we created a new one. I needed to keep the focus on my healing, to keep my heart and ears open to what God wanted to teach me. I had no control over the timing of the change that took place in Tim's life, and still have none today—I can only influence and pray for God to direct his steps.

Remember, you are working to reclaim your heart back to wholeness. Don't attempt to rush into the future, because that can feel like a daunting, impossible task. It's the little things that make the window clearer to allow God's hope to shine brightly in your relationship. Over time, there may be setbacks, but don't allow those challenges to wipe away your blessings and change your perspective of the future. Praise God for the crack in the window, the fresh air in your marriage, and the small God sightings in your relationship as He brings hope and healing to your heart.

I encourage you to put hope into practice and to name two blessings a day. This takes the focus off your pain and allows you to find traces of hope that will show up in your beautiful story. Everything around you may seem like it's falling apart at the seams and you may feel like you have lost all control of the situation, but I promise you, joy comes in the morning![2]

Cling to the promises God has given you that He will never leave you and will always love you in the good and the bad.

Reclaimed REFLECTION

What has hope looked like to you? Was it a person, a book, a rainbow, or something physical, like the affectionate brush of a shoulder, that indicated the road was turning upward?

Has it been hard to see through the smudges on the window? What do you do when you lose focus?

When the days are extremely dark and cloudy, are you capable of seeking out the blessings?

Reclaimed TRUTH

May your unfailing love rest upon us, O LORD, even as we put our hope in you.
Psalm 33:22

But blessed is the man who trusts in the LORD, whose confidence is in Him.
Jeremiah 17:7

"For I know the plans I have for you," declares the LORD, "plans to prosper you and not to harm you, plans to give you hope and a future." Jeremiah 29:11

Therefore my heart is glad and my tongue rejoices; my body also will live in hope.
Acts 2:26

 *Reclaimed* **PRAYER**

God, thank You for the sunrise and sunset today. For the details in the flowers, the majesty in the mountains, and the joy in the songs of the birds. May I never stop noticing You in all of creation or forget what You have already provided for me. God, help me to not lose hope because of my current circumstances. Guide my focus back to You, the provider and faithful Savior, who has not been void of my life this far. Amen.

Revival

If you saw the size of the blessing coming, you would understand the magnitude of the battle you are fighting.

—Stephanie Broersma

The Lord definitely did some major work on my husband's heart this week. There appears to be a breakthrough. However . . . my heart is so very cautious. There is a lot of fear still . . . but more hope than there has been in a long time. I am facing the sad reality of the future head on. I am no longer willing to pretend that we are "okay." I feel like I have wasted five years of my life . . . hoping and praying and believing that my marriage would be okay. But I am not willing to waste another five years, or even one year. I am going to step out with the Lord and allow him to lead and guide on this new path. I am trusting that He can use me in new ways, even though this is a path that I never dreamed of in my worst nightmares.

Krista

Have you ever been asked to do something you absolutely did not want to do? Something you attempted to avoid and escape from that made you dig your heels in deep into the ground? Jonah was that kind of person. He ran with every fiber in him to hide from the task the Lord assigned to him. Funny thing is, when you play a game of hide-and-seek with God, He'll find you, no matter what. Jonah ran from the Lord (Jonah 1:3) and ended up inside a great fish for three days and three nights until "the LORD commanded the fish to vomit Jonah onto dry land" (Jonah 2:10). It was then the Lord had Jonah's attention and the Word of the Lord came to Jonah a second time. This is the part of the story where Jonah brings revival to Nineveh and, after forty days, the Ninevites believed:

> The Ninevites believed God. They declared a fast, and all of them, from the greatest to the least, put on sackcloth. . . . When God saw what they did and how they turned from their evil ways, he had compassion and did not bring upon them the destruction he had threatened. (Jonah 3:5, 10)

I believe God sends people in my life to help steer me clear of danger and harm, like He sent Jonah to the city of Nineveh to warn them to turn to God. He sends me Jonahs in the form of parents, friends, mentors, and accountability partners, to grab my attention and encourage me to adjust my behavior.

Jonah was given a task to preach revival to a city that had lost its way and that was gripped in sin. If you ask Tim, there were people who were Jonahs in his life, too. People, songs, and messages he heard that encouraged him to get back on track.

But as with any sin, the Enemy is quick to tempt a person to reverse any progress, which then can cause a person to stumble and fall.

The stories women share with me about their husbands' falls no longer shock me. I've heard of wives being confronted by pregnant women carrying their husband's child. More than once I've witnessed financial security destroyed by years of fraud because of hidden sin. Jobs are lost because of inappropriate behavior in the workplace. Homes are foreclosed because fiscal responsibility is neglected. Men are so self-absorbed that they lose custody of their kids, resulting in grown children losing respect for parents. I've heard accounts where women went into hiding for their physical safety, and I have been asked to write testimonies for court documents about what I heard and saw. Most disheartening are the stories where men have turned so far from God—and their vows of commitment—choosing to pursue homosexuality, drugs, or finding a greater high, whether it be physical or emotional. Many men seek multiple women in an attempt to fill the voids in their lives. One woman disclosed that her husband molested her daughter in pursuit of his evil desire.

In all these horrific life-altering choices, what breaks God's heart the most are people who were once fully committed to Christ but now are driven by lust and addiction. This should break us like it breaks God's heart.

Scripture is clear how God feels about it when we turn away from him:

> The LORD is a jealous and avenging God; the LORD takes vengeance and is filled with wrath. The LORD takes vengeance on His foes and maintains his wrath against his enemies. The LORD is slow to anger and great in power; the LORD will not leave the guilty unpunished. His way is in the whirlwind and the storm, and clouds are the dust of His feet. (Nahum 1:2–3)

It breaks my heart when another wife is referred to me after she's been devastated by infidelity. To hear of children being split up and forced to take sides is the furthest thing from God's will for a family. Nineveh represents today's marriages. What God created and started in the garden, with intent and design, has turned into hearts growing cold and moving away from God. We have been given a guidebook on how to live holy lives. God promises an abundance of blessing for our obedience. Our sin has consequences, and the verses in Nahum are a reminder of God's patient love and His justice if we continue to follow our own selfish desires and ways.

> The LORD is good, a refuge in times of trouble. He cares for those who trust in him, but with an overwhelming flood he will make an end of Nineveh. (Nahum 1:7–8)

The betrayal you experienced is beyond a "time of trouble"—it is hell on earth. For many, nothing else compares to the empty feeling of being alone and stuck in the cycle of pain caused by sin. It can be hard to understand how God cares for you when you are in the middle of a crisis. He is good. He is faithful. He loves you and will not abandon you in your distress.

As women who seek wholeness for their heart, allowing the injury to initiate a revival will be like a flood of grace that spills over. One of my greatest joys is to hear of women using their stories of pain to bring hope to others in their own Nineveh season.

 *Reclaimed* REFLECTION

When have you ignored a warning against danger ahead of you? Did that result in physical or emotional pain?

Are you able to locate your own personal Nineveh in your life?

Do you have people in your life to hold you accountable and in line with what you want for yourself?

 ## Reclaimed **RUTH**

The LORD will restore the splendor of Jacob like the splendor of Israel.
Nahum 2:2a

The law of the LORD is perfect, reviving the soul.
Psalm 19:7a

Create in me a pure heart, O God, and renew a steadfast spirit within me.
Psalm 51:10

But you will receive power when the Holy Spirit comes on you; and you will be my witnesses in Jerusalem, and in all Judea and Samaria, and to the ends of the earth.
Acts 1:8

Reclaimed PRAYER

God, generate a spirit of discernment and surround me with wise counsel for all areas of my life. I give You permission to rid me of things causing repeat pain in my life and to do whatever is needed in order for me to see the potential destruction I'm allowing. God, I need a revival in my marriage, for my family, and for myself. Help me to receive Your love and not to get lazy in my quest toward healing. Thank You, Jesus, for rescuing me. Amen.

Stubbed Toes

Measure the size of the obstacle against the size of God.

—Beth Moore

I had little deaths along the way, finding pornography here and there throughout the years. Death of self-worth and image of myself . . . until God spoke to me and told me I was worthy. Death of loving myself as a daughter of Christ . . . until God told me I was loved. This was present all over the course of our marriage, not just recently. And the death of my family when my own parents divorced over pornography and affairs. Then the devastating death of our marriage in October, when I found out Michael had stepped outside our marriage bed. With that death, I experienced the different grieving stages that occur when someone dies. Looking back, I've gone through many of the stages already, without realizing them.

But the hope of the resurrection that God gives us through Jesus is the same hope I have for Michael and me.

Christina

One morning as I was opening the blinds and turning the lights on, I clumsily stumbled into the large table that has been sitting in the same place for years. It is beyond frustrating to stub your toe, and more so when something so small can create such agony. I had instant shooting pain and, within an hour, a black-and-purple pinkie toe. As I was icing my "serious" injury, I had an epiphany. Sometimes, the pain we encounter from stubbing our toes is like trying to dodge the sin in our lives. There are obvious places we know will cause pain, but we still run into them and stumble because as humans we are weak and far from perfect.

How quickly we forget the size of our God when in a difficult situation. We see the obstacles in front of us, feel the pain from the punches, and experience the emotional grief due to the sinful choices.

We focus on the initial pain and aren't capable of seeing past the hurt to envision the bigger picture. It's not until we take a step back that we see how we might have been able to avoid the pain, or see how God has been by our sides through every jab and punch that came our way.

It wasn't until I took a deep, honest look at my marriage that I noticed I wasn't practicing my husband's love language, which is physical touch. After years of feeling like Tim was not fulfilling my love language, which is quality time and words of affirmation, I had nothing to give back in return. I am a fixer and try to figure how I can do things differently, resulting in a more positive outcome. This is definitely an area I ignored, and I wished I would have done it differently, to avoid the pain.

My entire perspective has changed since walking the ugly road of deceit in my marriage. Often we don't make changes until we know something is broken. My plea to you is to learn your love language and strive to meet your husband's language in return so you don't have to experience the potential of a broken relationship and miss the bigger picture. I wish I saw the big elephant in my marriage years before having to experience the pain caused from not watching out and paying closer attention to something as simple as understanding my husband's love language. If I had seen what was coming, I would have sprinted in the opposite direction and done everything I possibly could to make things different.

My sister Traci was an example to me in what it looks like to keep your eyes on the bigger picture. Traci fought breast cancer for ten years, facing every challenge with an overcomer's spirit. Throughout the years supporting her during chemotherapy treatments, sending care packages, and shaving her head bald four times, one thing has stayed the same—Traci's attitude toward Christ. Her unwavering faith was rock solid in the many disappointing test results and discouraging lab counts. For as many times as the cancer returned, her faith doubled, multiplied in size, and her motivation to overcome that much larger! Praise God for her fighting attitude and ability to see the positive perspective amid a terrifying battle.

After spending a weekend together a few years before Traci passed, having some much needed sister time and deep conversation, she said, "What's the worst that can happen? I go home to heaven?"

The book *Hinds Feet on High Places* beautifully tells a story about "Much Afraid" and her journey to the high places.[1] Her story shares the peaks and valleys that were along the way as Much Afraid faced many obstacles in her quest to reach the highest. Inspired from the Scripture verse found in Habakkuk 3:19, which says, "The Sovereign LORD is my strength; he makes my feet like the feet of a deer, he enables me to go on the heights."

This verse is actually tattooed on my wrist, as it was my sister's life verse, which motivated her to continue to climb when her journey turned dark and scary.

As a trail runner, I have caught myself many times reflecting on this verse. When training for a race, I often stop to fuel up and grab a drink before setting out to run more miles. It's in these stops where I notice the little mountain flowers, the trickle of water dancing down the hillside, or the moss gracefully covering the branch of a tree, with vibrantly green ferns pointing toward the sky. If all I did was focus on finishing my run, then I would miss what God had created for me to enjoy and experience.

Perspective is what I have gained years after I thought I'd lost it all, insight into the many little details that make our marriage who we are—uniquely designed as individuals but also as one, a mountain that holds peaks and valleys, all handcrafted to point to the glory of God.

Marriage is a two-way street, and both people need to deposit as much love and devotion into the marriage as possible. It may take time to change our perspective on issues to see the bigger picture. We may need to be open to adjusting a few character flaws in ourselves to better the relationship—an extremely humbling experience, but one that needs to take place, as we should always strive to become better.

I'm thankful for God waking me up to see how I was not loving my husband as Christ commands me too. God has helped me to judge others less and to offer grace for those in need. And now I am aware of the obstacles that cause my husband to stub his toe, so to speak. I protect him, place barriers to steer him away, so our perspective can stay focused on the cross and us. I make it a prayer, as life continues to steam ahead, that my faith can stand firm in every situation and that I will see God in every challenge.

Whether it be fighting poor health, avoiding addiction, pouring into being a parent, or trying to pick up the puzzle pieces of your marriage, let God change your perspective so you can see all the glory in your story.

 *Reclaimed* REFLECTION

Has God changed your perspective on issues in your marriage?

What are you "stubbing your toe" on? Are there areas you need more cushion to protect your relationship?

What are some unexpected blessings in your journey of brokenness? Have you given thanks for what God has given you or spared thus far in your journey?

 *Reclaimed* **TRUTH**

I can't forgive myself and those who have betrayed me:
Therefore, there is now no condemnation for those who are in Christ Jesus.
Romans 8:1

I feel so alone:
The LORD God said, "It is not good for the man to be alone. I will make a helper suitable for him."
Genesis 2:18

This is too hard to deal with:
I can do everything through him who gives me strength.
Philippians 4:13

I'm afraid:
Even though I walk through the valley of the shadow of death, I will fear no evil, for you are with me; your rod and your staff, they comfort me.
Psalm 23:4

Reclaimed PRAYER

Jesus, it's hard for me to see past the pain and trauma I'm navigating right now. Give me Your eyes to see the beauty in my situation. Cause me to seek the blessings even though all I feel is heartache and trial. Guide me in this journey, and help me to not get stuck in the details but to focus on the victory You already have planned for my life. Thank You for preparing the road ahead when I can't see inches in front of me. You are so good, God. Thank You for blessing me with Your grace and love. Amen.

It Is What It Is

She stood in the storm, and when the wind did not blow her way, she adjusted her sails.

—Elizabeth Edwards

My husband's emotional growth is stunted by alcohol. I am struggling with the lies it took to get here. My codependency is like, "Yeah. You feel bad enough." My spirituality is like, "Change you, not him." And my brain is sometimes premeditating how to make it "look like an accident," while my heart is telling me that I love him so darn much, how could this happen?!?

Katherine

When I was in sixth grade, my parents had our first family meeting in the living room, and they explained that Dad had been diagnosed with colon cancer. Yes, I heard the words, but they didn't sink in until after Dad's surgery. Once the weekly routine of chemotherapy began, I had to accept the reality of the situation. In particular, the smell of nail polish reminded Dad of his treatments. Even today, I still think of my dad when I paint my nails, because it reminds me of when I had to accept that my dad was really sick.

Ten years ago I heard the same words, as my dad was diagnosed with cancer yet again. Then months later my sister was diagnosed with stage three breast cancer. When I stood by Traci's side in the operating room, whispering prayers of "I love you" in her ear, I was forced to accept the ugly reality of my sister being sick. She had to endure treatments and surgery alongside our dad. It was almost too much to accept.

No one wants to accept the truth of a cancer diagnosis. Words cannot express the depth of pain I felt, the loss and heartache for my parents and sister, and the support of friends surrounding us at the hospital the day my sister had her surgery. There was a questioning of our faith and uncertainty for the future as her body was altered in order to save her life. I was upset and dumbfounded at the thought of having to explain this situation to our oldest daughter.

Hearing the words "I slept with someone—I had an affair" are just as devastating as a cancer diagnosis. It sucks every ounce of air left in your body and numbs you to what is going on around you. Time froze for me, and if I were to move a step forward, I would then be forced to accept this new normal in my marriage and home. I wanted to go back and do everything all over again.

I eventually told my mom she could go home, as I needed to find a new routine on my own. The thought of possibly going back to work put me in a state of panic, as our kids were used to a stay-at-home mommy. The thought of moving to find a smaller apartment terrified me, as our home had been a sense of security. Accepting my new normal meant there were changes ahead that would make me uncomfortable—and it would demonstrate to others things were not okay at home.

I was faced with the grim reality of living with a spouse who was unfaithful. Just to make myself clear—God did not put me in this situation. Tim's choices led to me having to make life-altering decisions for our family. God gives us each free will and choice. He offers grace for the times we choose outside His will.

Two years post-confession, I struggled with the emotions of acceptance when Tim and I were on a trip to California. I was on edge the whole time. Traveling in general made me feel like I was forced to accept what had happened. I had fears of running into a woman who would recognize my husband. This made no sense to Tim, but he acknowledged my fears and how this was challenging for me. He gave me assurance, which calmed my anxiety.

Everyone chooses to accept their situation differently, but the truth is: *it is what it is!* We can't change what happened, nor the consequences that follow. As much as I begged God to heal my sister here on earth, His will already had ordained her days before He called her home to heaven. She often said that "it is what it is" throughout her years of treatment and even up to the last days of fighting the disease that consumed her body. I wanted God's will to be done in her life as much as I wanted to stuff the words back into my husband's mouth—but it wasn't God's plan.

God gives us earthly healing and heavenly healing, and we have no grounds to argue the outcome. He promises to be by our side either way, and He knows what we need to accept the truth and the new reality we will have to walk through.

When we get caught up in the details and our emotions lead the way, we tend to shut out the Holy Spirit from speaking to us. God's voice then becomes silent. The hardest part of betrayal is accepting that there *was* betrayal. Jesus knew ahead of time that Judas and Peter would betray Him, yet it still grieved Him greatly when it happened.

Nothing about your pain needs to be dismissed. Nothing about the heartache you're experiencing is easy. Acceptance is a part of grieving and is often the hardest step. Acceptance is challenging and emotionally draining, but it leads to the next step of healing and offers fresh hope in a somber situation.

I've seen acceptance take days for some women, and for others, years. Remember, every story is different and unique, so don't base your journey on the timeline of someone else's healing. Only you can determine what you need best—and God knows even more. Allow the Holy Spirit to give you clarity and wisdom as you navigate the steps of accepting what has happened in your marriage.

The sooner you can accept the "diagnosis," the sooner you can begin "treatments" to eradicate the disease that has taken your marriage hostage.

Reclaimed REFLECTION

Have you been able to fully accept the details of your spouse's unfaithfulness?

If not, do you see how that hinders your journey to healing? If yes, how have you seen God's hand of grace in the process of acceptance?

What fears do you have in regard to accepting the betrayal?

Reclaimed TRUTH

Accept one another, then, just as Christ accepted you, in order to bring praise to God.
Romans 15:7

The LORD has heard my cry for mercy; the LORD accepts my prayer.
Psalm 6:9

I tell you the truth, whoever accepts anyone I send accepts me; and whoever accepts me accepts the one who sent me.
John 13:20

For there are three that testify: the Spirit, the water and the blood; and the three are in agreement. We accept man's testimony, but God's testimony is greater because it is the testimony of God, which he has given about his Son. Anyone who believes in the Son of God has this testimony in his heart. Anyone who does not believe God has made him out to be a liar, because he has not believed the testimony God has given about his Son. And this is the testimony: God has given us eternal life, and this life is in his Son. He who has the Son has life; he who does not have the Son of God does not have life.
1 John 5:7–12

Reclaimed PRAYER

Jesus, I don't want to accept the pain and reality that confronts me, but I know I need to in order to find healing. With Your help, I humbly ask that You make my eyes see the truth, my ears hear confession, and my heart believe that it will get better. Go before me in my days as I explore the areas needing restoration. Gently massage truth into my wounds. Give me strength and endurance to fight my battles. Amen.

Protect Your Story

Therefore encourage one another and build each other up, just as in fact you are doing.

1 Thessalonians 5:11

I need help and am not sure where to turn. I feel so alone. I was told by my pastor that I just needed to have more sex with my husband and that would fix the problem. I have some family who say ditch him. Others are willing to do whatever they can to support us in making this work and really getting to the bottom of how we got here. My friends are wanting details, but I don't trust them, because I've seen what they do with gossip. This situation is isolating.

Sandra

Do you remember playing the childhood game "telephone"? You sit in a circle and start by whispering a statement in one person's ear. The next person passes the information to the next person until you reach the last person in the circle. By the time it reaches the other end, the statement is often twisted and nowhere near the first statement. It is hilarious to see how fast the story changes simply because people aren't carefully listening or are in a rush, and they say something backward. The same goes when you tell something in confidence to a friend. It always amazes me how quickly a story is distorted from the original version, or worse, if it's not protected by the original storyteller.

I once was told to protect my story, as it is only mine to share. When I felt safe enough and compelled to talk about our marital situation, I began to tell my story. Years after Tim and I went through our dark valley, the only people who knew about our struggle was our immediate family, pastors, and two close friends. I had a few clients who knew, but it was only because of my tears and needing to reschedule their appointments that they eventually found out.

In order to focus on us, we had to protect our journey by keeping silent so well-meaning advice and games of "telephone" wouldn't work against our progress. We surrounded our little family with those who would encourage, pray, and stand behind us in the trenches. Anyone outside of that closed circle would have been noise and a distraction from the hard work we needed to complete.

Jesus also had an inner circle of friends. He chose twelve disciples to share together and come alongside His ministry. If only we knew the conversations they shared around a fire or early mornings on their way to the next village. Jesus had words meant only for His disciples, as they lived in close communion with each other, and the mission He came to earth to accomplish was served through the close relationships He spent time building.

I've witnessed the horror that happens when an angry wife not only shares her husband's faults to her closest friends but then fires away on social media, thinking it will make her feel better. This is harmful because it allows others to take sides in a personal battle that needs to stay between the husband and wife. There's nothing encouraging or uplifting about sharing outside your inner circle. Doing so isn't anywhere close to exercising the integrity Christ asks of us in a crisis.

When broken women are stopped on the street by a "concerned friend" who only wants details on the juicy story rather than offering support, this is not helpful to your healing journey. Disclosing intimate details to those who don't care about your privacy is only going to lead to more hearsay and discouragement. When people talk, things get distorted.

Living in a small town, I've heard details about a marriage crisis become twisted with information from others, creating a different picture of the marriage, a picture that didn't exist. The sin of gossip runs rampant with the story. The result is broken wives having to deflect lies when confronted by complete strangers. This happens because people are curious and want to know the reason behind tears, separations, or conflicts. When you only hear one side of the story, it's easy to jump to conclusions. Most are not willing to listen to the other side, which creates dissension among families and friends.

Here is my strong encouragement: if you are not a part of the solution or the struggle, then it's none of your business, so please stop talking about other people. Sharing another's story that is not yours to share is the Enemy's greatest victory, as he splits families even further apart because of gossip.

I mentored Darlene for a few years. She was diligent to keep the focus on her character and allowed Jesus to reveal areas of growth she needed to work on. She had two kids and was consistent in counseling and extending forgiveness toward her husband, Frank. Her husband had even gone to rehab to address other addictions that fueled his affairs. They were doing great, until she listened to Shelley, a "friend" who thought she was being helpful. Shelley repeatedly told Darlene, "Once a cheater, always a cheater. You need to get out now before he loses this job."

The saddest part of the story is that Darlene listened to the unwise advice from her friend and not her inner circle, who had helped her to heal. The Enemy slowly worked to place hints of dishonesty toward her heart with Frank. As a result, their marriage that had been doing so well in recovery, ended in divorce. Darlene walked away from her faith because she listened to Shelley more than her wise counselors. Shelley told her to chase happiness and eventually encouraged Darlene to become involved in drugs and a lifestyle of one-night stands. An unplanned pregnancy followed, along with losing custody of her kids, and finally her family disowned her. All because she chose to listen to Shelley's unwise advice during a vulnerable time, and it eventually wore her down and interfered with the progress of her healing.

In order to promise wholeness in our marriages and in our hearts, we must speak the truth in love and seek godly counsel. It is important to protect not only ourselves from well-meaning friends but also to protect our spouses. In a moment of bitterness, it is easy to share to those around us how much of a monster we are married to and how awful we've been treated. If there is any chance of reconciliation, both parties must be cautious in their speech when sharing with others.

Praise God for our inner circle friends! My go-to gal came home with me just hours after Tim's confession. Tim sat in silence in the basement, not knowing where he was allowed to go. After picking up the kids from his grandma's, my girlfriend gave Tim a hug and assured him that we would get through this mess. Days later my mom also did the same thing as she embraced my husband and forgave him, without a shred of doubt that things would smooth out. Having the support of our church leaders was instrumental in our healing process, as they gave us the resources needed to sort through our emotions, the pain, and the consequences of the sin tangled in our relationship.

It became clear who we could trust with our story and who we could not. We confided in selected people who could handle the ugly details, and glossed over the particulars with others who could only handle the surface details. With everyone else, we kept our story quiet until we were strong enough to share publicly.[1] And even with our extremely small circle, we still had to deflect opinions of those close to us who thought we should handle things according to what they believed was best.

The more we share with others, the more opinions and judgments we will have to defend.

Over the years, trust has been rebuilt in our marriage by my knowing Tim has my back when I need him most. Being able to text him and ask for prayer or to share my struggles has been met with love and open arms. When he sees me broken and hurt, Tim is quick to offer up a silent prayer, as I need the outpouring of God's grace to get me through the day.

I know for a fact that our progress would not be this far without the support of so many people. Jesus is our main supporter, and we chose to surround ourselves with others who had the same values and the best interest of our marriage in mind.

Protect your spouse's story as well, as you heal and sift through information on the journey. Pray for each other to find the root of the pain and to communicate the emotions stirred up in the middle of those thoughts. Learn to lean on each other, as most likely the other is strong when you are weak.

Build alone time in your relationship, for you to process and seek God's best in your life. Find a mentor who can pour into your God-given gifts and encourage you to grow. Before attempting to care for those around you, sometimes the best idea is to take care of yourself first. God is your light and wants to bless you with immense support and unwavering love from the body of Christ. Lean on God's Word when all else fails—the most promising counsel will be found in the truths of the Bible.

🏵 *Reclaimed* REFLECTION

Are you taking measures to protect *your* story, realizing that your spouse's story is for him to share when he's ready?

Are you willing to have a mentor hold you accountable to learn how to speak your story appropriately? If not, why?

Have you been supportive and respectful of your spouse when sharing your story? If you were to ask your kids what your attitude toward your husband is, what would they say in a few words?

🏵 *Reclaimed* TRUTH

Never be lacking in zeal, but keep your spiritual fervor, serving the Lord.
Romans 12:11

Be wise in the way you act toward outsiders; make the most of every opportunity. Let your conversation be always full of grace, seasoned with salt, so that you may know how to answer everyone.
Colossians 4:5–6

Accept one another, then, just as Christ accepted you, in order to bring praise to God.
Romans 15:7

And let us consider how we may spur one another on toward love and good deeds.
Hebrews 10:24

 *Reclaimed* **PRAYER**

God, thank You for keeping my story safe with You. Give me discernment in whom I can trust with my shaky emotions and raw thoughts. Help me to reflect You through words and actions. God, if there is bitterness or resentment in my conversation, show me so I can change my voice to become more positive. I'm sorry if I have cast doubt in what You are capable of healing. Forgive me. Thank You for providing my circle of trust that encourages me to become better. God, You are so good. Amen.

Redeemed

Redeemed women of God have tender merciful hearts, backbones of steel, and hands that are prepared for the fight.

—Stasi Eldredge

Starting over again is terrifying yet exciting! It's the chance to give love another chance. In my marriage I had lost myself. This was the opportunity to get to know myself again and see myself through someone else's eyes. And the butterflies . . . falling in love again feels amazing. And if you are in a healthy God-driven relationship, you get to grow with someone in your faith and his.

I don't feel broken. I feel like I get to live again. And I have been given a second chance to be happy.

Gayle

We all like to watch movies or read books that have happy endings—a storyline where the bad guys get caught, a broken heart is mended, the sick are healed, and ugliness is turned into beauty. No one wants to watch or read a story where there is no redemption, no closure in the end. That's depressing.

I believe it's the same with our lives. We live in a "fix it" society where there are solutions offered for sale in any situation. The beauty of the cross is that God has given us an instruction booklet, the Bible, to follow and use as our guide when a happy ending seems far from reach.

As the grim reality of my broken marriage sank in, the idea of my relationship being restored never crossed my mind. All I could think about was the stinging pain from the confession and the need to remember to breathe—in and out. The pain consumed me. Praise God for grabbing me out of the pit of my personal hell and whispering to my soul. It was the little deposits of promises read in the Bible, and in the worship music I listened to that showed me the possibility of redemption. I had no perspective to hang on to at that time, so trusting in His Word became my nutrition and routine, assisting me as I navigated the deep waters of emotion.

Years later God has taken the good, the bad, and the ugly and redeemed them for His glory. God asked for my obedience to follow Him and to listen; therefore, rewarding me with a healthy marriage and longing for my spouse.

God does not waste anything! He wants his glory to be revealed in everything we do—even when there seems to be no happy ending in sight. Every tear will be wiped dry and vows recommitted in truth and in love, with a newfound intimacy. Sometimes it may be that the marriage is beyond repair, but God can still grant you a reconciled heart and give you redeeming qualities to share with others. Nothing is too far gone, too lost, for God to restore.

Remember, you too can be redeemed. When Jesus took our sins upon the wooden cross, we were forever redeemed. Forever saved from this ugly, fallen world we live in. Three nails, one in each hand, and one in Jesus's feet—and our lives were completely changed. In the moment of disbelief, you may not feel like anything can be redeemed, but that's what makes grace so beautiful. Trust Him; He sees what you can't see.

🪙 *Reclaimed* REFLECTION

God has a funny way of using our deepest flesh wounds to show His glory to others—but more importantly, to show us where our character lacks strength. How has God reconstructed your character and given you redemption through the pain?

What is the meaning of redemption?

Do you feel your story is worthy of being redeemed? Where is the fear stemming from if you feel undeserving of a second chance?

🪙 *Reclaimed* TRUTH

I have been crucified with Christ and I no longer live, but Christ lives in me. The life I now live in the body, I live by faith in the Son of God, who loved me and gave himself for me.
Galatians 2:20

Who gave himself for us to redeem us from all wickedness and to purify for himself a people that are his very own, eager to do what is good.
Titus 2:14

In him we have redemption through his blood, the forgiveness of sins, in accordance with the riches of God's grace that he lavished on us with all wisdom and understanding.
Ephesians 1:7–8

Worthy is the Lamb, who was slain, to receive power and wealth and wisdom and strength and honor and glory and praise!
Revelation 5:12

Reclaimed PRAYER

God, You are so sovereign. Your grace and mercy covers me daily, providing a fresh start every morning. Thank You for what was accomplished on the cross for me. In my emotional mess and confusion, You still stand firm as the rock of my life. God, I pray I never forget what it took to become redeemed. Show me how that can become possible in my broken relationships. Give me the ability to extend grace and mercy to others. Thank You for loving me always. Amen.

From Horror to Hope

There's not a chapter of our story that is authored by us. It's all written by the One who is the definition of wisdom, power, love and grace.
— Paul David Tripp

God made Jesus's resurrection perfect. I believe He can resurrect our marriage. The hope of the resurrection that God gave us through Jesus is the same hope I have for my marriage.

Andi

"*For this is what the* Sovereign LORD says: 'I myself will search for my sheep and look after them'" (Ezekiel 34:11). The first time I read this Scripture, it didn't sink in, but then I read it again, and the verse jumped off the page. Accepting the ugliness in my husband's life was hard to handle. I've compared the addiction to pornography in Tim's life to a cancer that spreads through a healthy body, sucking every living cell available in its path. The burning sting of pornography was more painful than the affairs that followed. It was like a venom that quickly paralyzed my mind and heart from believing I had any worth or value.

I was never going to be able to stand up to the pornographic airbrushed images and expectations.

The life was sucked out of me faster than letting go of a blown-up balloon, twisting and twirling around until completely deflated. My heart instantly was lost after Tim's confession, and the turmoil ransacked my mind. I found myself defeated.

I am forever grateful that God never let go of Tim's life, even when he chose to walk in sin, and He went searching for Tim when he was too lost to find his way home. In God's perfect timing, He plucked my husband out from the deepest pit he had thrown himself into, and God rescued him from the sin compromising his life. God knew how devastated I would be when I discovered Tim's secrets, and He did the same for me and rescued me by Hs grace. Instead of lifting me up to stand when I was crumpled on the ground, God gathered me in His arms and carried me. He covered me with His gentle feathers,[1] protecting me through the emotional storm that was to come.

Ezekiel spoke of God looking after his people and delivering a warm message and a promise to strengthen those who were scattered: "I will rescue them from all the places where they were scattered on a day of clouds and darkness" (Ezekiel 34:12).

God's promise of gathering His sheep is as true today as it was over two thousand years ago. When I read this, I think about how cloudy life is to people who can't find their way home because of sin. In my husband's case, he didn't realize he was lost until his heart was ready to listen. It was an opportunity for Tim's heart and mind to be open to hear God's truth about what the consequences would be if the trajectory of sin continued. God met Tim in his exhausted state and picked him up and bound his wounds. He offered Tim the freedom to move forward in his healing journey. God took the darkness away from my husband and protected his heart and mind, which only made him trust God more.

The addiction was gone. The need to pursue affairs and seek pornography was instantly removed, destroyed.

Ezekiel reveals the promises my husband experienced:

> There they will lie down in good grazing land, and there they will feed in a rich pasture on the mountains of Israel. I myself will tend my sheep and have them lie down, declares the Sovereign LORD. I will search for the lost and bring back the strays. I will bind up the injured and strengthen the weak, but the sleek and the strong I will destroy. I will shepherd the flock with justice. (Ezekiel 34:14–16)

God desires for us to find healing from all types of sin and pain. He promises us that if we rest in him, he will bind up our wounds and will destroy the lies around us. What hope this is, especially when we struggle with a burdensome secret of darkness that steals from our marriage!

I wrestled with unbelief in the months that followed Tim's confession. *Am I stupid for thinking we can make this work? Will he pursue lust again, making me look like a fool for staying committed to the marriage?* It was only by faith that I took the first steps to see that God truly did want to rescue and provide for me on my journey. There is nothing that compares to the blessing that comes when I choose to trust God. The following verse gives me comfort:

> I will make a covenant of peace with them and rid the land of wild beasts so that they may live in the desert and sleep in the forests in safety. I will bless them and the places surrounding my hill. I will send down showers in season; there will be showers of blessing. (Ezekiel 34:25–26)

Recently, I met with Holly, a beautiful bride who experienced many painful situations in her marriage, stemming from her husband's addiction of pornography. After several lengthy discussions, prayer, counsel from their church, and complete surrender to each other, Holly found safety in God's protection and a new covenant with her husband.

For Holly, it meant having her husband write down every sexual sin that was done against her, and then she prayed over each line, forgiving her husband for every single act. At that point, she crossed each sin out, blotting it out, erasing it from the list. She set herself free from the bondage of the past but also allowed her husband to see true forgiveness in her heart. Afterward, they signed contracts with each other as a form of accountability. Everyone deals with crises differently than their neighbors, and some need more accountability than others. I found what this renewed couple did to be 100 percent honest, but profound as well. To some, it may seem extreme, but when the network of sexual sin has you paralyzed, you need stern accountability to hold you true to your vows. God will rid your life of the wild beast of whatever sin you're dealing with and will send down showers of renewed blessings.

I had to know every detail of Tim's affairs in order to not create fantasies of what might have happened outside of our marriage. Let's face it—Hollywood has turned the idea of an affair into a dream vacation. Knowing the details helped me to forgive not only my husband but also the women involved in my husband's sinful web. (Some women are not capable of handling such details. If you know you won't respond well to all the details, then please, for the sake of your heart and mind, don't ask for them. I suggest you boldly ask God to remove the need for information.)

God is in the search-and-rescue business. He promises when we hit rock bottom and have nowhere to go but up that we can rely on Him. Yes, my pit came through my husband's confession, but I am so thankful I was able to look up as my Shepherd went looking for His broken, wounded daughter. It took a tangled web of lies, betrayal, and shame to finally wake Tim up and accept the glorious riches of following Christ. God has given me a breathtaking pasture of hope and belief filled with intimacy, restored vows, and a forgiving, Christlike attitude toward my husband. And as I take in the beauty in front of me, I get to do that hand in hand with my husband, my lover, in our redeemed marriage. I embrace the time in our pasture and rejoice that He is our God!

 *Reclaimed* REFLECTION

Are you lost? Are you aware of why God is searching for you? Have you confronted the sin in your life?

Can you recognize the showers of blessings God is providing for you?

How have you been able to rest in the pasture as God binds up your wounds?

 *Reclaimed* TRUTH

You are my sheep, the sheep of my pasture, and I am your God, declares the Sovereign LORD.
Ezekiel 34:31

Reclaimed **PRAYER**

Jesus, thank You for searching for me when I didn't realize I was lost. Show me what I need rescuing from as I wander in what feels like a lost and vacant desert. Direct my steps to the living water You freely offer. I pray my heart is soft enough to receive the knowledge You want to download to my soul. Help me to never forget Your Word and truth. Open my eyes to see the blessings You hand placed in my life to brighten a dark day. Jesus, You are such a giving God. Amen.

Waiting for Tomorrow's Sunrise

The best we can hope for in this life is a knothole peek at the shining realities ahead. Yet a glimpse is enough. It's enough to convince our hearts that whatever sufferings and sorrows currently assail us aren't worthy of comparison to that which waits over the horizon.

—Joni Eareckson Tada

God has been reminding me of how far he's taken me and telling me again . . . chosen. God continues to choose me in so many different ways and offering situations where I need to reciprocate and "choose" His direction and promptings. Last year I never would have thought I'd/we'd be where we are now. And sometimes I just get emotional and overwhelmed with gratefulness! (And it comes out in eye leaking!) I keep praying God continues to reveal those deep-rooted hurts that drive the "escape" button without actually hitting that button. They seem to take a long time to work through and discover, but as time moves forward, I see more hope of restoration.

Annie

Telling someone whose life is in shambles to "just have hope" is a loaded statement, when all around them life seems to be falling apart at the seams. I catch myself saying "Hope you have a good day" or "Hope you feel better" quite casually—a surface statement that usually carries no weight in word or deed. Try saying that to someone whose life is lived in a wheelchair, or to a couple striving to have a family. *Merriam-Webster* defines *hope* as "a feeling of expectation and desire for a certain thing to happen, or a feeling of trust. Hope is a desire, a wish, an aspiration for something more, a goal, or plan. Hope is a verb; our faith being tested for what we cannot control."[1]

The catalyst for our brokenness doesn't have to be devastating, though sometimes it is. Suffering comes in all sizes and shapes every day of our lives. And when it comes, we often bury the pain somewhere deep inside us. It simmers and stews, gnawing away at our peace, turning our hearts cold against any glimpse of experiencing hope again. The real tragedy is when we can't see past the crumbled mess of our brokenness to look into the face of Jesus and worship Him.

I recently read about a young couple who struggled with revisited addictions and failures over the course of eight years of marriage. This broken wife's husband had a sex addiction, and early in their marriage, he violated their vows multiple times in unimaginable ways. Hope seemed impossible as this wife endured trial after trial and became desperate to see a glimmer of hope for the future. It finally came after both filed for divorce, and God showed Himself in powerful ways in the midst of sin. It took a sliver of hope to rebuild this marriage, and praise God, this couple stands strong and is experiencing blessing for obeying and following God's Word.

During the raw moments of my husband's confession, I never imagined I'd gain a single grain of hope in our marriage. How in the world could God take this disgusting situation and turn it around for good? I saw no hope for reconciliation or for a future together. The emotions of the present clouded the possibilities for tomorrow. But God shook me upside down and gave me a tiny breath of fresh air through a cracked window. In the conversations just days later, Tim and I were able to speak more clearly than we had ever before in our seven years of marriage. When all I wanted was to take him to the ground and beat him, God gave me control of my words, respect in my heart, and honesty in my thoughts, and He showed me where I needed to believe Him and build character.

During one of these conversations, all I wanted was a hug—the need for touch and intimacy was strong—and yet I despised him. I hated him in that moment and yet couldn't let go. God showed me I still loved this man who'd wrecked me so deeply.

To me, hope is God taking the impossible and helping us believe what's possible. I hoped for my two-year-old to potty train herself, for my house to magically clean itself, and for my laundry to fold and put itself away. (Can I get an *amen* from some young mamas?) I hope for cancer to flee from my vocabulary and healthy cells to flow through the veins of those plagued with the disease. I hope for my children to find godly men and women to marry someday. I hope for Christ to come and save me from more pain before I experience it.

Hope is real. Hope is within our reach, and God wants us to hope with great excitement and to place our hope in Him alone. It's what gets us to take that first step toward forgiveness, reconciliation, and sometimes that first hug we crave so intensely. Hope should be a part of a believer's DNA. Let us not forget it when life is completely out of control. "I wait for the LORD, my soul waits, and in his word I put my hope" (Psalm 130:5).

In seeking hope, we need to also recognize there will be continued disappointments. Brokenness will still follow us, and our times of experiencing pain is not over. Psalm 77 speaks about this and is marked by a sense of inward trouble and reflection, temptation and darkness.

In the first few verses, we read about a sorrowful, deserted soul walking in darkness—which isn't common among those who fear the Lord. The psalmist Asaph found himself in such need that he was physically stretched out with his hand laid before the Lord, crying out to God for comfort and mercy.

I related to Asaph in the days after Tim's confession. Paralyzed by the fear of our future for our marriage, I too was with hands outstretched, begging God to take my pain away. I found myself asking God why He allowed this to happen and how He could let Tim fall so far into sin that it would destroy me and the kids. I was angry, embarrassed. I felt shame for my husband's sins, violated by the filth that entered his mind and slipped past his hands.

The night of the confession, I yelled at God for what I was experiencing, complaining in complete brokenness and trying to find a person to blame for this mess. And then, much like the psalmist, I had an awakening that translated my fears into hope. It happened when I stepped back and remembered what God had done and was doing in my life. It became an antidote against the darkness that plagued me day and night. God's promises became a sanctuary of goodness on some of the hardest days. "I remembered you, O God, and I groaned; I mused, and my spirit grew faint. You kept my eyes from closing; I was too troubled to speak" (Psalm 77:3–4).

Starting in verse 10 of Psalm 77, we see the transition where Asaph begins to remember those good works: "Then I thought, 'To this I will appeal: the years of the right hand Most High. I will remember the deeds of the Lord; yes, I will remember your miracles of long ago. I will meditate on all your works and consider all your mighty deeds" (Psalm 77:10–12).

In the English Standard Version, the verse reads, "I will remember your wonders of old." And in the New Living Translation, "I recall all you have done, O Lord." *But then . . . enter hope!* The "but then" is an important part of our brokenness. It is the point of transition from sorrow to joy. The point where we see our need for God versus being stuck in our pity and ashes. Asaph made a conscious decision to turn from his pain and rather focus on the wonders of God.

There were days when the pain of my husband's sin was so thick and heavy that I could only see what was right in front of me: my own pain and my needs. I didn't have the strength to seek God in the moment, because of my own weakness sucking the very breath from my lungs. I had nothing to offer besides my devotion to God. It was when I allowed myself to rest completely in His strength that my eyes started to see the blessings still being poured into my life.

Instead of a trickle of truth, God substituted my pain and replaced it with hope. When I switched my focus to seeking blessings rather than what was horribly wrong, my heart danced a little, I smiled more, and finding contentment in my pain was easier to accept.

 *Reclaimed* REFLECTION

Is your hope in God? Do you believe He will overcome your pain?

Does your brokenness control your attitude?

What are two blessings in your life right now?

🌐 *Reclaimed* TRUTH

Find rest, O my soul, in God alone; my hope comes from him.
Psalm 62:5

Not only so, but we also rejoice in our sufferings, because we know that suffering produces perseverance; perseverance, character; and character, hope.
Romans 5:3–4

I have told you these things, so that in me you may have peace. In this world you will have trouble. But take heart! I have overcome the world.
John 16:33

I cried out to God for help; I cried out to God to hear me. When I was in distress, I sought the Lord; at night I stretched out untiring hands, and I would not be comforted. I remembered you, God, and I groaned; I meditated, and my spirit grew faint. . . . Then I thought, "To this I will appeal: the years when the Most High stretched out his right hand. I will remember the deeds of the Lord; yes, I will remember your miracles of long ago. I will consider all your works and meditate on all Your mighty deeds."
Psalm 77:1–3, 12

Reclaimed PRAYER

Thank You, Jesus, for giving me eternal hope! I know this is all temporary, but I need that additional push of encouragement to believe it will get better. Jesus, my hand is outstretched, begging for something good to come out of my situation. I ask You be with me in my fear and doubt. Help me to not get hyper-focused on the negative details but to rather place my sight on my eternal home. I rest in You, God, Amen.

DAY 25

Joy

Joy is the serious business of heaven.

—C. S. Lewis

For the first time ever in my life, I feel full. I have never in my years felt such peace and overflowing joy from walking with Jesus. I had to sell my house, I had to find a new job, and our divorce was just finalized, but I'm still smiling. It is only because of Jesus.

Allie

When life is in line with God's Word, we should experience joy every day. I have a passion for running, and I find joy when I can get lost on the trails and allow exhaustion to set into my lungs. I find pure delight when my children snuggle up, wanting nothing more than my attention and affection. There is excitement watching the spring buds appear on the trees and bushes as new beginnings burst forth in the sunshine. Nothing compares to the joy that fills your heart as you meet your newborn baby for the first time. In all our joy, we must never lose sight of Who gives us that ability to experience joy.

In marriage, we can experience joy by simply having fun. This was a concept Tim and I lost sight of over the years of striving to meet our goals, but the moments we did have were over the top. Our joy was found in more grown-up ways, such as completing a remodeling project, landing a big job, or expanding careers and hobby accomplishments, but either way, we did have fun and have now learned to work on giving our marriage margin to create joy. Our kids often have puzzled looks on their faces because of the inside jokes we share when we laugh together.

It takes discipline to set aside time to date each other and to show our young families what joy in a marriage looks like. Even when the life hits the pavement and we're in the midst of a rough patch, we are still encouraged by God to find joy.

Over the years, I have seen the devil rip marriages apart and steal a couple's joy. I've witnessed people choosing bitterness versus forgiveness, then realize that the grass is not greener on the other side. I've seen a well of emotions reappear thirty-five years after a betrayal, pain caused from the lack of grace given. I've observed generations suffering from selfish decisions, with joy buried because facing truth is too hard.

The devil is having a party as he brings chaos to our marriages and casts a sky of despair to those too weak to fight the battle. God challenges us to find joy in our trials because He knows that it will build character and make us stronger. I can now say I find joy in our valley, as it has proved to me how strong I am, how strong my faith is, and how strongly I believe in our marriage. It's the "glass half-full versus half-empty" concept when viewing a challenge.

In the Old Testament, we see joy associated with true worship of God. During King Hezekiah's reign, the Israelites rededicated themselves to God and the people renewed their commitment to God, which reignited the joy in their hearts.[1] In the New Testament, Paul experienced joy by simply doing God's will in his ministry; he encourages us to find joy in Christ's sufferings.[2] James tells us to "count it all joy" when we are facing trials or are in the midst of suffering.[3]

The only thing that can steal our joy is sin. By encompassing your life with His Word and His truth, you protect yourself against the flaming arrows that want to rip away the smile and destroy the joy that is promised to us. Allow the joy to shine through to the outside, and let others see the beauty in the ashes as God restores your heart and heals your wounds.

 *Reclaimed* **REFLECTION**

In Isaiah 55:12, we are told to "go out with joy and be led forth in peace." Have you been able to follow through with that command as you face personal struggles and hardships?

What things bring you joy from sunrise to sunset?

Are you afraid to find joy again fearing something bad will happen again? What attempts have been made to seek joy?

Reclaimed TRUTH

Consider it pure joy, my brothers, whenever you face trials of many kinds, because you know that the testing of your faith develops perseverance.
James 1:2–3

My lips will shout for joy when I sing praise to you—I, whom You have redeemed.
Psalm 71:23

Those who sow with tears will reap with songs of joy.
Psalm 126:5

When times are good, be happy; but when times are bad, consider this: God has made the one as well as the other.
Ecclesiastes 7:14

Reclaimed PRAYER

God, my joy comes from you even though my heart feels shattered and marriage undetermined if it will ever be restored. Open my eyes to see what brings you joy. I pray I never become too calloused that I can't find You in creation or my family that surrounds me. I pray my words bring cheer to those around me. God, help me to laugh again and find the activities that bring me into a time of fulfillment. I demand all depression and negativity to flee from my entire home. Help me to resist the darkness and speak with authority in my life. Give me overwhelming joy and peace in my life. Amen.

Beauty from Ashes

You don't have the luxury of planning even the next sentence to come out of your mouth. You immediately publish the distempers or radiancies of your soul. You publish by the questions you ask (or don't ask), by how you listen (or don't really want to listen), by the interpretations you offer (or don't even think to offer), by the advice you give (or can't give), by the attitude you take toward people, toward problems and toward people with problems.

—Dr. David Powlison

God, in His timing, can take the ashes of our grief and brokenness and make them beautiful. The ashes that once burned with lifeless hope of renewal and a million questions has become fertile ground where fruit is planted and a foundation is being established. None of this is mine and Paul's doing but God's work within two imperfect people. I am still fragile, but I can trust my unknown future, in the hands of an all-knowing God. I have faith that from these ashes our God will make our marriage beautiful.

Ellen

My dad has had a project growing in the garage for over thirty years. I'm pretty sure it sits on four wheels and resembles the form of a car, but to me I see twisted and distorted metal that desperately needs a paint job. Some parts are where they belong in the engine, but there are also car parts to the '64 Chevy Impala in closets and, once, under my bed when growing up. Every year Dad goes down south to a car show, picking up a few more parts for his prized hobby car. He hopes that someday his beauty will be polished and he can drive his bride through town.

In 2009 I felt like my marriage was just like Dad's hobby car. I didn't recognize it under all the dents and missing parts from the pain and scars of betrayal. I had all the tools at my fingertips: pastoral counseling, marriage books, podcasts, repentant husband, and supportive friends and family. But in order to turn ashes to beauty, you have to put the time and work to get to the finished product.

My dad has never been in a rush to fix his car. It gives him something to tinker on when he has time. I didn't have time to loiter and be idle about fixing what was broken. I had to make a choice to either sit in pity or attempt to put the pieces back together, knowing it was an uphill battle. I thought I knew what it was going to take in order to make the marriage work—but never expected the emotions involved or the blessings that would come from a restored marriage.

Once I shared with Tim that divorce was not an option, I could see relief wash over him. But there was also fear of the unknown path of healing. I remember asking our pastor if there was a handbook that could tell me what to do in order to repair our marriage. Tim was willing to do anything at this point, but I was still walking on eggshells with unstable emotions. Choosing to mend the marriage meant that I also chose to not look back.

Everything I did was with the intention to make us better, stronger, and more willing to expose anything in our relationship that would sour and spoil our future. Tim and I devoted every evening (once the kids were in bed) to read together, talk together, and listen to as many marriage podcasts and watch as many DVDs as possible. We met with pastoral staff to help direct us to the right people who could assist us in diving deeper into our issues. Tim and I met separately with counselors, and we had a team of close friends and family who held us up in prayer and encouraged us with no judgment.

In biblical times, people built a hedge of thorns around their gardens and even their houses as an effective method of protection. Likewise, we need to build a hedge of protection around our marriages. "Have you not put a hedge around him and his household and everything he has? You have blessed the work of his hands, so that his flocks and herds are spread throughout the land" (Job 1:10).

We must agree to not take any chances with our marriages when trying to protect and restore what is broken. Part of the hedge is found in education and proper support and counsel, and the other is cementing your faith in the one who can restore even the ugliest of sins. This was something Tim and I had to relearn, even though the truth was not far from us. Tim's faith was being rediscovered, and he had a new fire growing inside him. I clung to my faith, and it was the only thing that kept me alive.

Part of our restoring process was learning as individuals to depend solely on God, and then together as a couple. God has done a beautiful remodel of our marriage—one that I never knew could exist. We have open communication and can blurt out anything without judgment from the other.

There is a new sense of urgency to be with each other, whether sitting in silence reading books, walking hand in hand at the park, or working outside together on yard projects. God has given us a platform to come alongside other hurting couples and mentor and encourage them as they navigate through uncharted waters. Restoration has led us to a new love for each other—a love that is firm in our faith, grounded in the cross, and ready for whatever else comes our way. The hedge around our home is much taller, able to protect our family from all the flaming arrows the devil throws our direction.

So whether it's an old, ugly, beat-up car that promises to someday be a cherry-red, shiny beauty or a marriage that's frayed, tattered, and tired, with the right amount of attention, determination, and prayer, it can be restored.

Rebuilding a marriage is not a quick repair and paint-job restoration. Nothing that lasts happens overnight, and with time, God will reward you for the decision to choose healing.

God desires for your heart to find wholeness, and that may mean you walk the rest of the road alone. He will grant you the patience needed as mistakes are made and change is sought. God is not quick to judge, and He wants you to follow His example when you confess to one another and seek transparency in your relationship. You might not see progress when compared to the day before, but over time, you will see, with God's help, a beautifully restored and reclaimed you.

First restoration steps:
- Summarize what you are restoring; ask God to bring all that needs mending to the surface, followed by forgiveness.
- Pray, asking God to comfort you both and to give you listening ears as you seek restoration.
- Own 100 percent of the 1 percent that is yours to own.
- List what you need to make restoration possible.
- Be firm, but also know you may need to compromise.
- Boundaries—they need to be tested. Set dates to achieve goals, tasks, and needs.
- Forgiveness.
- More prayer.
- More forgiveness.
- Reevaluate the situation if it's not working.

Reclaimed REFLECTION

Do you feel you have the tools necessary to remodel your relationship? If not, have you found the courage to speak up and ask for help?

What are some ways you have restored your marriage and God has healed your heart?

Are you able to locate your healing in the steps listed above for restoration?

Reclaimed TRUTH

He restores my soul. He guides me in paths of righteousness for his name's sake.
Psalm 23:3

Restore to me the joy of your salvation and grant me a willing spirit, to sustain me.
Psalm 51:12

If we claim that we're free of sin, we're only fooling ourselves. A claim like that is errant nonsense. On the other hand, if we admit our sins—make a clean breast of them—he won't let us down; he'll be true to Himself. He'll forgive our sins and purge us of all wrongdoing. 1 John 1:9 (*The Message*)

After Job had prayed for his friends, the LORD made him prosperous again and gave him twice as much as he had before.
Job 42:10

 *Reclaimed* **PRAYER**

Father God, thank You for sustaining me all this time as I learn more about myself and who I am as Your daughter. Keep my words gentle, my boundaries firm, and my heart aligned with You. Thank You for making my broken parts whole again and showing me that they have purpose as You restore my life. Your blessings brighten my day like the promise of a rainbow in a blue sky. Let me see You in every part of my life. Amen.

The First Kiss

Most marriages start in the wrong place because they start with happiness as the goal. God did not create that as the goal; that was supposed to be the benefit.

—Tony Evans

There are moments where I crave a simple touch, and at the same time, my stomach revolts to think of being physical once again. My emotions contradict themselves, and the feeling of being completely lost paralyzes my judgment and thinking. Thinking of being physical again repulses me and also intrigues me. I question all my relationships and don't feel safe even in my own home. The betrayal left me numb to any feelings, hunger pains, or sense of urgency toward anything. I feel trapped at the bottom of a steep well . . . alone.

From Stephanie's Journal

Tim and I were separated for ten days. We would pass each other in the driveway at the end of the day, avoiding any physical contact or obligation to talk to each other. The arrangement was such that Tim would come home for the evening routine as I would go do something else for three hours—then, the kids now tucked away in bed, we would once again pass each other in the driveway.

One of those nights, I asked Tim to stay so we could talk. After getting the youngest to bed, he found me sitting on the couch, worship music in the background, and silent, torturous tears streaming down my cheeks. I hurt so bad, and now that the kids were in bed, I didn't have to worry about hiding my pain. I found it weird to sit on the couch together, so—making it more awkward—we sat on the floor as we opened some exposing topics.

Three hours into the uncomfortable conversation, I badly craved a simple hug. I missed our nightly snuggles and getting tangled up in bed together. In the seven years we had been married, we'd never stopped playing footsie in bed. We'd always held hands and showed affection. The lack of any affection was another reminder of what we'd both lost. When I asked Tim for a hug, his distant embrace was physically distressing, yet gave me a strange twinge of hope.

After four weeks of sleeping on the couch, I decided to try the bed again. Sleeping like I was in a stiff straight jacket, I managed to find anything but sleep. After more processing, I invited Tim to join me—still not encouraging him to make any advances toward me. Eventually, we held hands and finally had our first kiss.

The first time we were intimate, I wept. I had it in my head that by allowing us to become intimate again, I was somehow accepting his unfaithfulness and all the pain that was wrapped in that moment.

Then there was the experience of having to visit the doctor to be tested for STDs—explaining to the doctor why it was that I wanted every test possible. I wanted to be sure I had no physical evidence of his unfaithfulness—I felt like I was sleeping with the other women and with every image my husband ever laid eyes on that should have been directed only to me. It was so unbearable.

Not all stories are like this. I've sat with women who crave physical touch more than words of affirmation. Some don't want to face what their reality will be like, so it's easier to keep to the same routine, offering more sex as a way to keep their husbands attracted to them. It is a sad, destructive cycle. David Powlison wrote a book titled *Making All Things New: Restoring Pure Joy to the Sexually Broken*. He says this about the context of being sexually broken:

> Sex is one good strand of God's good work in creation. Sex is one good strand of His good work in salvation. Many people experience pain and fear attached to sexual victimization. Sex becomes like a life in Auschwitz, like a burn survivor, a walking nightmare of hurt, fear and helplessness from the hands of tormentors. Jesus' kindness redeems both sinners and sufferers. The erotic is meant to be a bright expression of mutual loving kindness. Sex thrives in a context of commitment, safety, trust, affection, giving, closeness, intimacy, and generosity.[1]

God wants to redeem this area in our lives. Sex is not meant to be painful or done out of routine. It's to be alive and active, full of intense passion, and can be fully brought back to life if given the attention our intimacy deserves. As brides, we are worthy of being cherished and loved, desired and needed.

After Erica's affair, she lost all hope to ever have a healthy marriage again. With countless prayer and endless work by both her and her husband, they now have a healthy sex life, in which she tells her husband "thank you" during some of their most intimate moments.

Whether you are at the stage of feeling disgusted by looking at your husband or are a few years further down the road because healing has taken place, we should first tell God "Thank You!" for what He created. We need to find the rare blessing in our marriage sexuality that so often is the root cause of our pain.

Reclaimed REFLECTION

What fears do you have regarding becoming intimate once again with your spouse?

If the marriage ended in divorce, have you thoroughly processed the pain so you can have a fresh beginning with someone else?

Are you able to locate the triggers within intimacy so that you can restore the wholeness of what God intended for man and woman to experience?

Reclaimed TRUTH

The LORD God said, "It is not good for the man to be alone. I will make a helper suitable for him."
Genesis 2:18

May your fountain be blessed, and may you rejoice in the wife of your youth.
Proverbs 5:18

Whoever does not love does not know God, because God is love.
1 John 4:8

Let him kiss me with the kisses of his mouth—for your love is more delightful than wine. Pleasing is the fragrance of your perfumes; your name is like perfume poured out. No wonder the young women love you!
Song of Songs 1:2–3

 *Reclaimed* **PRAYER**

God, part of me is embarrassed to even pray for this, but You know my thoughts and anxieties. God, I need You to help me start over, even with cuddles and kisses. Create in me a new passion for my marriage and husband. Spark an intimacy between us while keeping my heart focused on You. God, I invite Your spirit to fill my home as I begin to offer my heart to others. Protect me as I try to love again. Amen.

Do We Tell the Kids?

Children have a wonderful way of discerning the truth . . . even when we think it's being hidden.

—Fred Rogers

Our kids are really shook up after talking to their dad in rehab. We've been forced to tell them basic details since much of this mess is public. I wish I could have protected them from this pain, much less myself. This has forced them to grow up years in advance.

Tess

There's no cookie-cutter answer for whether or not you tell your kids or keep the pain secret. Our oldest was not quite five years old, and one was still in diapers. No books we've read say that there is a right time or age that you should tell your kids what happened in your marriage.

I know of grown children who to this day have no knowledge of their father's infidelity. On the other hand, I know of children as young as four who have been thrown into the ugly mess because of domestic violence and because law enforcement needed to get involved to prevent further abuse.

I've helped protect wives who went into hiding with their children, watching their entire worlds turn upside down. The important fact to remember when you consider telling your kids is that it should come from a parent—one who can gracefully and age appropriately explain the situation, with only enough details so that the child is not harmed. Nothing is more devastating than to hear about their parents' troubles from friends or family members they don't trust.

Tim moved out for our brief separation. My young children saw me physically upset and the people who came to check on me, and they would ask why I was crying. Knowing they would not understand anything about betrayal, I simply responded by stating I had a friend who was sick, which made Mommy very upset.

The funniest explanation came from my girlfriend, when her boys wondered why I was bringing my laundry to her house and was always in tears. Tim's confession had come at year seven in our marriage, the "seven-year itch" or, in this case, the time when everything broke down. It just so happened that our toaster, coffeepot, and Crock-Pot all died within weeks of the separation. Then followed the washing machine—which was the reason I had asked my girlfriend for help with a few loads of dirty clothes. To this day, those sweet boys still think all my tears were because my washing machine died!

It wasn't until this past year that we told our oldest daughter, now a teenager, about Daddy stepping outside the marriage. The conversation wasn't planned—rather one that just fell into the nighttime routine of saying our prayers. When asked what she knew about betrayal, it was clear she grasped the definition. There were no details given about the choices Tim made—just that he had stepped outside our marriage and betrayed Mom. She had a few questions, and we reassured her that forgiveness was extended and that we loved each other very much. Our daughter is very mature for her age, and we didn't expect anything other than an accepting response.

Most affairs are not random. They're between friends or people who are familiar with each other. This produces tension among friends and acquaintances.

For other women, that's not the case. When Amelia told her high school–aged kids that their dad had an affair, it was met with extreme distaste, as they had already heard ugly rumors. The unfortunate part to this story is that the other couple involved was not as protective with the details and these rumors had already hit their teenagers.

Amelia was forced to defend her kids and went all-out mama bear to those trying to pry information out of her kids or call them names meant for the betrayer. Her husband not only needed to rebuild Amelia's trust but also that of his kids, who were seriously disgusted by the rumors and lies.

On the flip side are the wives who put all their energy into protecting their kids from the truth. Arizona did so much to protect the truth that it's been fifteen years of covering up her secret pain to keep anyone else from knowing about her husband's infidelity. Maggie caused herself years of torture simply because she wanted the kids to graduate from school before she filed for divorce—something her husband requested many years earlier but she just couldn't because there was always something she wanted to wait a little longer for: a graduation, a wedding, a grandchild, or another major life event. The emotional pain was extended and drawn out, which should have ended years earlier, all because of her tremendous fear in telling her kids the marriage had failed.

One benefit of telling your kids is the opportunity it presents to explain how to guard yourself against the Enemy's temptation to sin. He wants nothing more than to highlight your weaknesses, so using this moment to teach your kids—regardless of their age—about how to protect their eyes and minds against lust is a perfect reason to share. Yes, it puts you in an extremely vulnerable position of exposing the sin that entered your home, but the benefits outweigh the fear. The sin is exposed and restoration is visible, and although the children may not understand everything, they can witness the healing process, which in turn can influence their choices in the future.

We've done this with our son, teaching him to respect himself enough to avoid lust of the eyes. We've taught him about inappropriate images that could pop up on his electronic devices, and we've explained why we have parental-control apps. Many other parents have done the same, and the results are amazing.

A close friend who understands the deep despair of betrayal did this very thing with her young son. Leah discovered her husband's ruthless addiction that was stained with emotional and physical affairs, all stemming from internet connections. This had been going on unnoticed for ten years, causing Leah to pack up immediately following the discovery and to go into hiding for four months before considering moving back home. It's hard to distract young kids from why Daddy's not around when it's more than a week; even a few days can be a challenge. Leah had no other option than to explain what was going on to her young son. What she did best was explain the sins committed, using the Word to teach him that lust of the eyes is wrong. She gave him tools to assist him as he grows and gracefully taught him that what he pursues now will ultimately affect his marriage later.

There is no easy way to tell your kids. Prepare yourself for a few different reactions. Much like adults have coping mechanisms and different responses, so will your children. You may have the kid who takes sides and runs from you emotionally. Some kids distance themselves by focusing on school and friends so they don't have to be at home. Other kids have a look of numbness that doesn't go away; they internalize their emotions and have no opinion on anything, just "I'm fine."

Whatever the reaction, you should be prepared for the potential emotional fallout. Many kids feel like they need to take sides. Some turn to the world and seek revenge or attention through relationships, becoming sexually active because "If Mom and Dad can't keep it together, why should I?" The best advice I can share with you is to use this opportunity to teach your kids. "Yes, your earthly parents will fail and let you down, but your Abba Father, your heavenly Father, will never disappoint you, fail you, or cause any such pain."

Using this time to direct their pain and confusion and to point them back to God is huge. I've witnessed entire families become stronger all because they sought their Abba Daddy rather than focus on the failures of their earthly father. I've seen families rise up from the shattered pieces of suicide because of infidelity and dedicate their lives to Christ. Profound healing takes place all because Jesus, the only person who has not deserted them, is standing by their side as the waves rage around them.

Because you are their parent, you will know what is right for your kids. You know what they are emotionally capable of handling. Only one of our children know the surface details, but all of them understand Mommy leads small groups for women and sometimes has to talk in private when someone is hurting. Why? Because God has ignited a purpose in me I didn't realize until after I experienced my own personal hell. And when I had the strength to stand on my own two feet again, I stood and walked forward with humility, an abundance of compassion, and a desire to extend forgiveness to others. Your kids will be given an opportunity as they discover their parents' failure, and God will rush to their side and comfort their pain and confusion.

Reclaimed REFLECTION

Have you experienced honest conversation with your kids when discussing the status of your marriage?

If there are children in the home and they know what's going on, how have they reacted to the betrayal? Do you notice bitterness or any of the kids taking sides?

What have you done to reassure other family members that it wasn't their fault this happened and to make sure they know they are safe and loved and that it's safe to speak to you if the need arises?

Reclaimed TRUTH

Above all, love each other deeply, because love covers a multitude of sins.
1 Peter 4:8

Be kind and compassionate to one another, forgiving each other, just as in Christ God forgave you.
Ephesians 4:32

Honor your father and your mother, so that you may live long in the land the LORD your
God is giving you.
Exodus 20:12

"Honor your father and mother"—which is the first commandment with a promise.
Ephesians 6:2

Reclaimed **PRAYER**

God, I need You to help me be the best parent I can when all around me it feels like a swirling tornado. Use me to be a solid place of security and comfort for my kids. Protect their eyes and ears from conversations that are beyond their understanding. Silence my words if I become bitter around them, and cause my speech to be filled with grace and humility. I pray our children run to You and that this draws them closer to Your Word. My prayer is that we all become stronger—please help us to listen to Your voice and lean on You. Amen.

Keeping It Vertical

Your most profound and intimate experiences of worship will likely be in your darkest days—when your heart is broken, when you feel abandoned, when you're out of options, when the pain is great and you turn to God alone.

—Rick Warren

Nothing makes any sense to me right now except for my relationship with Jesus. It's the only constant that hasn't changed when all else is falling apart.

Kayla

In my journey of pursuing God and inviting Him into my deepest pain as I seek continued healing, I've come to realize that people are going to disappoint me. Failure from my own expectations and those that others create waste my emotional energy. And the time spent in anger and frustration sometimes destroy relationships. But the disappointment in my marriage far outweighs any other failure.

To best understand disappointment, we need to know what it means. *Merriam-Webster* defines disappointment as this: "Defeat or failure of expectation or hope; miscarriage of design or plan; a feeling of dissatisfaction that follows the failure of expectations or hopes to manifest."[1]

Failure—something we're all familiar with. Loss—we've all experienced it. No one wakes up and says, "Wow, today I'd like to experience some disappointment. I'd like to navigate through some failure and taste defeat." How absurd would that be? Nowhere in my right mind did I ask or want Tim to come home and reveal all the dirty secrets he'd kept from me. One comfort I've held on to through this journey is that God is familiar with disappointment. We read about the first disappointment in Genesis 3:6–24, when Adam and Eve sinned against God. God's heart was broken, his perfect creation marred by sin. The first and one of many disappointments we find in the Bible, and yet God's loving grace and mercy are woven through each story. We will experience disappointment in our expectations for our husbands, for ourselves, and for God—and none of them should be of any surprise to us, due to the unattainable goal of perfection.

Here are a few disappointments and unmet expectations I've experienced:

Disappointments in marriage:
- Rushed financial decisions that had great impact on our future endeavors.
- The expectation of living in one place, because that's what I experienced growing up, turned into moving three times before finding "home."
- A lack of affection during one of my pregnancies that brought self-doubt and shame.
- Expectation to read my mind and know exactly what I'm thinking so he knows how to act around me.

Disappointment involving others:
- Expectation of people being emotionally and physically available when we needed them to be.
- Expectation of our kids being healthy, obedient, and successful.
- Expectation that adoption would be easier (but it is hard). Disappointment in our birth mom caring enough to protect our daughter during pregnancy.
- Expectation in job security, health, and friendships.

Ultimate disappointment in my marriage:
- Disappointed that Tim didn't value our vows enough to cherish and protect our marriage.
- Disappointed that from his confession on, I had to live with the weight of sin and the consequences and the failure to remain faithful.
- Disappointed from the expectation to not have sin tempt my husband and to think it wouldn't taint our lives.
- Disappointed in myself for not protecting our marriage, seeing the signs, or knowing the pornography was present, and mad at myself for not being more sexual, more confident in who I was.

It is imperative we understand that the Enemy is ready to attack and consume anyone who has their guard down. The more I strengthen and grow my relationship with Christ, the more the devil gets ticked off and works overtime to get me to stumble.

We read about Job's friends in the Bible, who are referred to as "brothers" being like dry streams.[2] At one time, when Job was suffering, his feelings of disappointment were intensified because of the endless unhelpful conversation from his friends. When Job's life was good, his friends were good friends—but when Job had troubles, they could not help him. We see in Scripture that Job compared his friends to torrents of water that pass away in the summer, a seasonal stream that vanishes in the time of greatest need.

The idea of having people meet your highest expectations will be of no help because humans are terrified of illness, pain, and loss. As we consider all we have faced since betrayal entered our marriages, consider the one relationship that has never—nor will it ever—disappointed you this side of heaven—Jesus.

By striving to keep your heart aligned with Jesus, we gain support to help fight against the multitude of disappointments in our lives. But if the heart motive is not aligned with God's Word, there is no place we can run that will fulfill the need or the expectations we are seeking. Charlotte, who had attended the Reclaimed small group, was completely and utterly devastated by her husband's unfaithfulness. She felt she was failing miserably, trying to fix her kids' relationships with their dad, making amends with her friends, and attempting to keep herself together. It was almost comical, as she simply couldn't understand why things were so hard for her when she was rightfully pursuing peace. She was saying the right things and wasn't retaliating with brutal words, and she had been quite humble throughout the process up to that point. Yet she still was completely broken and found no blessings or good coming from her situation.

After talking with her further, I finally asked her about her relationship with the Lord. Where was she putting her trust? What was she doing to make God the primary focus in her broken mess? She simply hung her head low and said, "I put myself in the driver's seat and can't seem to release control back to Jesus."

If our vertical relationship with Jesus is not solid, then nothing productive will happen with our horizontal relationships. We can't pour into others if we're not allowing God to pour into us.

I have fought disappointment in my marriage by looking upward. Easier said than done, especially in those first few days and months after confession. But even years later, when there are times of weakness or frustration, I rely on Jesus first. I had to realize that I was not capable of handling any of my burdens alone. That was the hardest battle, releasing control back to God. Terrifying! I also had to remember that I am just as capable of disappointing others and need as much grace as the sinner next to me.

 *Reclaimed* REFLECTION

How do you deal with unmet expectations? What does God say about disappointment?

Are you secure in your vertical relationship with Jesus? Do you often reach out horizontally when needing help, instead of reaching toward Jesus?

Can you recognize these disappointments within your marriage?

Reclaimed TRUTH

And hope does not disappoint us, because God has poured out his love into our hearts by the Holy Spirit, whom he has given us.
Romans 5:5

They cried to you and were saved; in you they trusted and were not disappointed.
Psalm 22:5

For God so loved the world that he gave his one and only Son, that whoever believes in him shall not perish but have eternal life.
John 3:16

The name of the LORD is a strong tower; the righteous run to it and are safe.
Proverbs 18:10

Reclaimed PRAYER

God, thank you for pursuing me. I pray that I never place myself over Your authority in my life. Provoke me into a right relationship with You. Help my eyes to look upward instead of on my own intentions and desires. I know You see me, God. Assist me in maintaining focus vertically on You regardless of the chaos around me. You are a just God. You have been faithful to me. Thank You for guiding me thus far in my life. Cause me to pursue more of You offering a deeper relationship with my Savior. Amen.

DAY 30

Starting Over

Dust doesn't have to signify the end. Dust is often what must be present for the new to begin.

—Lysa Terkeurst

Our marriage has never been full, and I'm not sure what it'll feel like when it is. I'm scared but excited at the same time.

Stacey

A few days before a race, and often right up to the starting gun signaling the beginning, I often find myself getting the jitters, the type that make my adrenaline go off the charts and my stomach swirl.

After a few miles, everything settles: the pace, my breathing, the cadence of steps. If you blitz at the start line and exert all your energy at the beginning of the race, you'll find yourself depleted of strength to finish the race well. The key to any long-distance runner is to set the pace in the first couple of miles so your body can sustain the distance.

I've participated in many races of different distances, and there's always one runner who takes off like a rabbit—the overzealous, hyper-confident athlete who is more concerned about winning the medal than the accomplishment of competing fairly. Most runners have a finish time in mind, and they set training goals months prior to accomplish a personal record. Strength training, coaching, and good nutrition are all part of getting your body race-day ready.

Starting over in your marriage mimics the same training schedule of a distance runner. We have the goal of achieving wholeness and reconciliation, which requires two willing spouses who are repentant and forgiving of each other. Two willing marriage athletes who are ready to put in countless hours of brutal cross-training, stretching of muscles, and the long runs that cause your body to become fatigued and sore. With the proper support from a training coach, the goal of a restored marriage can easily be conquered—not! I think it's more like a strenuous, non-GPS hike up the side of Mount Everest.

Listen to what my favorite verses from the Bible says on this subject:

Not that I have already obtained all this, or have already been made perfect, but I press on to take hold of that for which Christ Jesus took hold of me. Brothers, I do not consider myself yet to have taken hold of it. But one thing I do: Forgetting what is behind and straining toward what is ahead, I press on toward the goal to win the prize for which God has called me heavenward in Christ Jesus. (Philippians 3:12–14)

I have fought the good fight, I have finished the race, I have kept the faith. (2 Timothy 4:7)

There will be days when you simply don't want to continue the process of pursuing healing. The faintest glimpse of reconciliation is so far off in the distance that it seems impossible to continue. Thoughts of fatigue make room for doubt and seeds of mistrust to be planted, which in turn uproot any progress you've made thus far.

The hardest part of starting over is the fact that we know we can't go back to old habits. What we did before is now completely off the table. Many who find themselves divorced have said this is the biggest challenge for them because they compare the previous marriage to a new and current relationship, which ends in disappointment from unmet expectations. Thinking we can do the same thing over again and have a different result, living with the same sin cycle, is absurd. Something has to change.

Angela attended the Reclaimed Small Group and found herself trying the same thing for five years to kick-start her marriage into restoration. Nothing about their lifestyle changed after her husband, Derek's, confession of an emotional affair. There was no accountability in the workplace, no follow-up to a one-time marriage counseling session, and no heart change that would result in permanent changes. They continued with the same dance they were sidestepping before the confession.

If it's not working, start again and try something different!

Angela and Derek needed to find a new dance. If you find yourself in the position of listening to the same content from a counselor, with no growth as a couple, maybe it's time to graduate to another counselor who can best meet your needs. Before you switch, I suggest analyzing your heart condition to see if the reason why there is stagnant growth is possibly because you are not willing to change.

It's like me trying to attempt a long-distance trail run wearing soccer cleats and never understanding why I have such horrible blisters and injuries. If I never stop to assess the situation, then I'll never figure out the solution. This goes back to knowing your "why."

The why—I'm not wearing proper running gear. The solution—I need trail shoes, proper socks, and a hydration pack to nourish my body for the race. To wear soccer cleats again and again would be foolish. It is the same in pursuing wholeness after betrayal.

As you consider starting over, remember this: God, not your husband, is your source of strength. God has given your husband to you as a gift. Your happiness comes as you begin to seek joy and create new memories, but happiness should not be your strongest or only motivator.

Tim and I still find ourselves staring at each other, asking for do-overs, a moment to rewind the clock and say this or that over again without offending the other. We still have mentors walking with us, coaching and encouraging us as our journey continues forward.

I still have a stack of marriage books I read regularly to gain more knowledge about the marriage we continue to mold. Starting over is exciting, inspiring, and worth every breathtaking view God chooses to bless us with if we're willing to tie our shoes tightly, put on the proper gear, and get ready to run the most critical race of our lives.

That's not to say we haven't had setbacks or injuries—we have. Temptations give in to triggers that get me in a funk, causing distance and frustration. Many times we've had to stop and realize we need to start over from the beginning again to allow more healing to spring forward. Not a failure, not a detour, but part of our journey toward full redemption, which can't be obtained until we reach heaven.

When we consider starting over, it is a race where the finish-line reward is wholeness, which rewards us with medals around our necks, displaying to everyone we have been reclaimed by God's grace and never-ending love. That medal demonstrates the skills of forgiveness, reconciliation, and the ability to overcome impossible assignments and to conquer the Enemy with victory for the incredible progress we've made together.

Reclaimed REFLECTION

What fears do you have to consider again?

Are you having to start over again after a divorce? What steps are you taking to keep things vertical?

How have you seen your extended family support you as you begin again? What are a few things they have done well in supporting your decision to start over?

Reclaimed TRUTH

To bestow on them a crown of beauty instead of ashes, the oil of joy instead of mourning, and a garment of praise instead of a spirit of despair. They will be called oaks of righteousness, a planting of the LORD to display his splendor instead of your shame, you will receive a double portion, and instead of disgrace, you will rejoice in your inheritance. And so you will inherit a double portion in your land, and everlasting joy will be yours.
Isaiah 61:3, 7

Forget the former things; do not dwell on the past. See, I am doing a new thing! Now it springs up; do you not perceive it? I am making a way in the desert and streams in the wasteland.
Isaiah 43:18–19

He who was seated on the throne said, "I am making everything new!" Then he said, "Write this down, for these words are trustworthy and true."
Revelation 21:5

Behold, I will create new heavens and a new earth. The former things will not be remembered, nor will they come to mind.
Isaiah 65:17

Reclaimed PRAYER

Jesus, You know my fear as I start over with a brand-new relationship. Allow my heart to expect good things, and let my eyes not see the scars all the time. Give my spirit excitement in this new season. Jesus, if my heart is not right, encourage me to repent and see that it may be me in the way of Your blessings. Thank You for renovating my thoughts and relationships, letting go of control, to release Your will in my life. Restore my heart to full awareness and abundance of blessings in Your truth. Give me a spirit of joy as I start over. Your grace sustains me. Amen.

Moving Forward

There was nothing more terrifying than having to realize the journey it would take to fix my marriage. If there was one lesson God taught me repeatedly, it was to rely on Him first and only. Everything else was out of my control. There was nothing I could do more or less to take this addiction away from my husband or make him desire me more. The only person I could change was me.

As you continue to pursue healing and wholeness, please remember this one thing: you can only change yourself. You can't fix your husband. You will eliminate so much extra burden when you can see that the only change possible begins with you. It starts with accepting the gift of the cross and asking God to reign in your life. To fully confess of your sin and allow Jesus's forgiveness of your sins to wash you whole and clean.

The reason you may have picked up this book is because you might be in a difficult marriage. There was a moment sitting in my pastor's office when I asked if he had a handbook for those experiencing betrayal, a step-by-step—on this day do this, and the next day do that—kind of book. Sadly, there wasn't at the time, and besides, every story is different.

Let me offer a few practical steps as you face the road ahead of you: Seek Help. Trust God. Plug In.

1. **Seek help** from professionals. If you need to speak to a counselor, ask your local church for a list of Christian counselors you can contact. You may need more intense therapy, such as rehab or a marriage retreat, which can focus on specific areas in need of restoration. Reclaimed also provides Small Group materials for churches. If you feel this resource would be helpful for your church, please visit www.reclaimedministry.com/church-support, fill out the form, and we will provide them a free Reclaimed book and Small Group resources for their consideration, so other women can find healing and help in this critical moment.

2. **Trust God** even when your world is crumbling around you. The Holy Spirit is with you, and when invited into your mess, He is ready to fill the physical void you're experiencing and can replace it with great joy.

3. **Get yourself plugged in** with those willing to support, laugh, cry with you, and speak wisdom to your soul. Betrayal is lonely. One of the most basic human responses to pain is to run and hide, to turn in to yourself and hug your pain close. Now is the time to break that cycle and make the decision that you are willing to share your pain with others who truly understand. If you don't feel you have a safe, trusted person to share your hurt with, please contact me through the website: www.reclaimedministry.com.

Lastly, I pray for abundant blessings and God's richest goodness over your story. I pray for God to provide all the resources and needs you desire as you seek to restore all that is broken.

I still feel hurt some days, and the triggers remind me of the pain of the past, but I choose to focus forward, always keeping my eyes on Jesus.

The Lord bless you and keep you; the Lord make His face shine on you and be gracious to you; the Lord turn His face toward you and give you peace.

A Word of Encouragement to Broken Wives

I historically take a backseat in Reclaimed Ministry, as let's face it, by default I am consistently front and center in much of the materials and content. I believe most men feel this same desire, to stay out of the light as they dive into the process of healing and restoration in their marriage.

Why do they feel this way?

God built us to be courageous, confident leaders for our families. Over time, this strength and courage can morph into a pride issue, which becomes the primary motivation for our fall into sin and addiction. Addiction, in general, is born from a place of pride and the need to be in charge. So once a man discovers his addiction and works on healing, he can have a fear of stepping back out and leading again. Fear that as he leads, he will find himself proud of his efforts. Fear that he may not be strong enough to overpower the devil's use of his pride against him. And in the end, fear that he will fail once again.

When I confessed my sin of addiction to Steph, the burden of failure, fears, and embarrassment all left, and I felt a great sense of relief. Whether a man is caught or chooses to confess, he bears a heavy burden for his lies and behavior. The burden eats at him, and after a while, even if he is enjoying the addiction, he feels the weight of his choices. He also feels shame and guilt when he looks at you, his wife. He doesn't know what to do with it, so he buries the shame and guilt. Your husband lives with self-imposed walls to protect himself from the discovery of the lies he created from the addiction.

When the walls come down and he is finally relieved of his burden, it's arguably one of the most freeing moments, and one that I will never forget. For the first time, I felt like I was able to dive into the next round of my growth and healing, my development as a husband, father, and son of the Most High God. I was not only excited to experience new growth, but I was eager to work on this part of my life.

My healing catapulted to the next level when my wife started walking the road with me. I acknowledge that early on, when the pain and confession are fresh, it may not yet be possible for a wife to walk that road with her husband. But when you can identify that your husband genuinely wants true healing and help, the sooner you become his partner in it, the better.

I vividly remember business trips where I would call Steph and share with her how I was struggling. She met me in those moments with grace and compassion. She asked me what my plan was to avoid temptation, and her tone was layered with empathy and not guilt and shame. I know this was brutally hard for her, but it was one of the biggest catalysts of my growth. It helped me to keep the walls down. Although there were consequences, forgiveness, grace, and compassion were still present.

Remember, your husband is afraid of failing again, and he fears pride taking over. He needs assurance that you, as his partner, support his efforts at recovery

I share all of this with you as an encouragement to stay the course and don't give up. Remember, your husband's recovery is his responsibility. Never forget that you, as his wife, have a tremendous influence on his journey. By no means does that imply you take the lead. He alone needs to lead his recovery effort.

Hang in there, ladies. If your husband is sincerely repentant, then he is worth fighting for. God can and will use this to shape both of you for years to come. We are fervently praying for your restoration!

Tim Broersma

Acknowledgements

Reclaimed: Finding Your Identity after Marital Betrayal
was birthed from a multitude of emotional coffee dates with broken
women—women who have experienced betrayal similar to mine and who
continue to pursue healing. To God be all the glory in the many stories
He continues to mold into greatness. For each hurting wife who trusted
me with her story and allowed me to walk alongside her, I thank you.

Tim, my love and my husband. Without your confession, we would
not be who we are today. Tim, thank you for your obedience to confess,
your willingness to listen to God's voice, your choice to become accountable, and your steady love when I am unlovable. Thank you for loving
me during my ugly moments and accepting the space needed to take
back our marriage. Thank you for giving me full transparency into your
heart and mind so that I could learn to trust and love you more than I
ever thought possible. You and me, my love. You are the leader Jesus has
always wanted for our family, and I'm truly honored to be your bride.

Pastor Kim and *his wife, Anne Ryan*, thank you for being incredibly
bold yet gentle mentors in our lives, both before and after the confession.

Your grace and ability to speak truth into my life that first night changed the tone of my marriage.

Mom and Dad, thank you for never judging or pointing fingers when things all fell apart. Your sacrifice to love me unconditionally has been a remarkable example of Christ's love. I will forever appreciate all the moments you held me when weeping or gave me room to process as you graciously cared for our kids. I'm so grateful for your continued active role in their lives. You are my inspiration. I love you both so very much.

Catherine, my friend and sister in Christ, thank you for catching me minutes after Tim's confession, even with all the snot and tears of confusion falling to the floor. Your immediate willingness to hold my hand through such intense moments spoke to me of forgiveness and humility. Thank you for our times in search of God's beauty near your home and for encouraging me to build in self-care. Your prophetic word over my life continues to become reality. I am forever grateful for our friendship.

Pastor Kurt, the support and words of affirmation you have given toward our ministry and our marriage have been exceptionally powerful to both Tim and me. Your honesty, messages of truth and hope, and your friendship are never taken for granted.

Ramona and *Michelle*, thank you for your constant encouragement and gentle nudge to turn this study into a reality. Your support in the ministry has been unwavering.

And to all our other *family and friends*, thank you for your constant love and forgiveness toward me, whether you knew my story or not. To those who cried with me, cheered me with countless hours of support, and prayed quietly when you knew I was weak, thank you.

About the Author

Stephanie Ann (Van Dyken) Broersma, a hairstylist by trade, is now a stay-at-home mommy to four little blessings. Married since 2002, Tim and Stephanie find new ways to enjoy intimate time together while raising their young family. She enjoys coffee, trail running, scrapbooking, being outdoors in her garden, and any opportunity to share a meal with a friend or with family. Stephanie and her family live in the Northwest pocket of Washington state.

Visit www.reclaimedministry.com to read more about Reclaimed Ministry. Join the closed group Reclaimed Ministry Community on Facebook, follow Stephanie Broersma, or follow us at @reclaimedministry for ministry updates and to stay connected.

*Photo credit by Jodi Van Straalen and the SNAPsisters Photography, www.thesnapsisters.com.

Reclaimed Small Groups

Reclaimed small groups are small, confidential, multi-church groups that meet to walk through the topics found in the *Reclaimed: Finding Your Identity after Marital Betrayal*. These intimate groups provide close accountability with other women in similar situations. The groups offer support, understanding, and encouragement as we work through the twelve-week course.

The groups have no homework but do provide suggested reading of articles, Scriptures on which to meditate, and personal reflections to discuss together or privately. Much like *Reclaimed: Finding Your Identity after Marital Betrayal*, the focus is always on the vertical relationship with Jesus Christ. A companion resource, *The Reclaimed Blessing Journal*, provides you a place to write your thoughts and take note of daily blessings, along with prompting questions and Scriptures on which to reflect.

The *Reclaimed Leader's Guide* and the *Reclaimed Workbook* are additional tools available. Visit www.reclaimedministry.com for more information and to purchase Reclaimed products, and see where a small group meets near you.

Related Materials

Reclaimed Small Group Leader's Guide
Reclaimed Small Group User's Guide
The Blessing Journal

Endnotes

Day 1

1. J. Allan Peterson, *The Myth of the Greener Grass* (Tyndale House Publishers, 1984), 111.

Day 2

1. Tim Jackson, "When a Spouse Is Unfaithful," *Our Daily Bread*, 1999, 2002. Our Daily Bread Ministries, Grand Rapids, Michigan. Reprinted by permission. All rights reserved.

Day 5

1. Neil T. Anderson, *The Bondage Breaker* (Harvest House Publishers, 2006), 222–224.

Day 6

1. *Merriam-Webster Dictionary*, https://www.merriam-webster.com/dictionary/shame.
2. Christian Jarrett, "Does This Brain Research Prove That Humiliation Is the Most Intense Human Emotion?" May

5, 2014, https://www.wired.com/2014/05/does-this-brain-research-prove-that-humiliation-is-the-most-intense-human-emotion/.

3. Brené Brown, *Rising Strong* (Random House, reprint edition, April 4, 2017).

Day 7

1. Beth Moore (Bible study), *Sacred Secrets—Study Journal: A Living Proof Live Experience* (LifeWay Christian Resources, 2015).
2. "Oh Be Careful Little Eyes What You See" (Zondervan Music Publishers, 1956).

Day 8

1. Gary Chapman, *Desperate Marriages* (Northfield Publishing, 2008), 180–181.

Chapter 13

1. "Hymn Story: Trust and Obey," sermon writer Richard Niell Donovan, 2007, https://www.sermonwriter.com/hymn-stories/trust-and-obey/.
2. "Trust and Obey" lyrics by John H. Sammis (1846–1919), music by Daniel B. Towner (1850–1919); public domain.

Day 14

1. *Who We REALLY Are—Our Identity in Christ*, GreatBibleStudy.com, http://www.greatbiblestudy.com/who_we_really_are.php.

Day 16

1. "Porn Stats (2018 Edition)," downloaded from the Covenant Eyes website, www.covenanteyes.com/pornstats/.

2. "The Most Viewed Porn Categories of 2017 Are Pretty Messed Up." *Fight the New Drug*, https://fightthenewdrug.org/pornhub-reports-most-viewed-porn-of-2017/ (accessed May 21, 2018).

3. Paul M. Barret, "The new republic of porn," *Bloomberg Businessweek*, June 21, 2012, https://www.bloomberg.com/news/articles/2012-06-21/the-new-republic-of-porn (accessed June7, 2018).

4. Maryam Kamvar and Shumeet Baluja, "A Large Scale Study of Wireless Search Behavior: Google Mobile Search," *CHI 06: Proceedings of the SIGCHI Conference on Human Factors in Computing Systems* (2006), 701–709, http://www.kevinli.net/courses/mobilehci_w2012/papers/googlemobilesearch.pdf (accessed June 7, 2018).

5. "A Marriage Revived, *The Broersma Five*, October 1, 2015, https://thebroersmafive.blogspot.com/2015/10/a-marriage-revived.html.

Day 17

1. Joshua 6.
2. Psalm 30:5.

Day 19

1. Hannah Hurnard, *Hinds Feet on High Places* (Ellie Claire Gift & Paper, 2015).

Day 21

1. To watch the Broersma's testimonies visit:
   • Tim's Story, https://vimeo.com/23924178
   • Stephanie's Story, https://vimeo.com/24592854
   • CBN 700 Club, https://www.youtube.com/watch?v=a340_we_KDw

Day 23

1. Psalm 91:4.

Day 24

1. *Merriam-Webster Dictionary*, https://www.merriam-webster. com/dictionary/hope.

Day 25

1. 2 Chronicles 29–31.
2. Philippians 1:12–30.
3. James 1:2–3.

Day 27

1. David Powlison, *Making All Things New: Restoring Pure Joy to the Sexually Broken* (Crossway, 2017).

Day 29

1. *Merriam-Webster Dictionary*, https://www.merriamwebster.com/ dictionary/disappointment.
2. Job 6:15

Order Information

REDEMPTION PRESS IP

To order additional copies of this book, please visit
www.redemption-press.com.
Also available on Amazon.com and BarnesandNoble.com
Or by calling toll free 1-844-2REDEEM.